# HEFT ON WHEELS

**Also by Mike Magnuson**

*The Fire Gospels*
*The Right Man for the Job*
*Lummox*

# HEFT ON WHEELS

*A Field Guide to Doing a 180*

# MIKE MAGNUSON

THREE RIVERS PRESS • NEW YORK

Published in the United States by Three Rivers Press, an imprint of the
Crown Publishing Group, a division of Random House, Inc., New York.
www.crownpublishing.com

THREE RIVERS PRESS and the Tugboat design are registered trademarks
of Random House, Inc.

Originally published in hardcover in the United States by Harmony
Books, a division of Random House, Inc., New York, in 2004.

Portions of the work have previously appeared in slightly different form in
*GQ* and *Bicycling* magazines.

Library of Congress Cataloging-in-Publication Data
Magnuson, Mike, 1963–
    Heft on wheels : a field guide to doing a 180 / Mike Magnuson.—1st ed.
    1. Magnuson, Mike, 1963. 2. Cyclists—United States—Biography.
    3. Dieters—United States—Biography. 4. Bicycle racing—Training—
    United States. I. Title
GV1051.M37A3        2004
796.6'2'092—dc 22        2003028092

ISBN 1-4000-5241-6

Printed in the United States of America

Design by Leonard Henderson

10 9 8 7 6 5 4 3

First Paperback Edition

*To Elizabeth Rose Magnuson*

Special thanks to the following:

Backroads Active Travel

*Bicycling* magazine

Caldwell County Chamber of Commerce in Lenoir,
North Carolina

Carbondale Cycle

Litespeed Bicycles (American Bicycle Group)

Cathy Rhuberg

Joe Shrader at Bird's Eye View Photography

Southern Illinois University Cycling Club

Team MACK Racing

Greg "The Animal" Wilson

# ACKNOWLEDGMENTS

I'd like to thank the following people without whom this book would not be possible.

Lisa Bankoff, literary agent, who has never told me that cycling is crazy. Thanks so much, Lisa, for your continuing patience.

Teryn Johnson, editor, who has cracked the whip and helped me to believe in myself again.

Thanks to all the cool people at Harmony Books, particularly Shaye Areheart, Kim Kanner Meisner, Tara Delaney Gilbride, and Bill Adams.

My daughters, Anne and Helen, real troopers.

My wife Elizabeth, to whom I dedicate this book.

My mother-in-law, Freda Barbeau, who has been such a great help to our family so many times.

Dr. John Foster and Dr. William Turley and Dr. David Anthony.

And Dr. Clarisse Zimra. It's really your fault, Clarisse; you arranged for me to ride with those guys in the first place.

Thanks especially to the Wine Trail Maintenance Crew: Darren Sherkat, Mike Pease, Tony Steinbock, Don Mullison, John Reimbold, Heston Roop-Duval, Gerald Schumacher, Ben Miller, Thomas Price, Loren Easter, Goeff Maring, Christina Cannova, Rachael Cunnick, Stephanie Grant, and Kristen Carter.

And whatever happened to Matt Gindlesparger? Or

# Acknowledgments

Ed Erickson? Or Alan "Farm Frites" Wagner? Or Brad and Melinda? Or the oldest cyclist in the world, Jeff Bell?

And Dr. Fred, what are you still doing on that recumbent?

Thanks to everyone at Carbondale Cycle, especially Choak Samkroot, Chris Norrington, Brendan and Mary Collier, Alex Reyes, and Scott Schnaufer.

Thanks, too, to Gary Doering at Team MACK Racing Association.

And finally, I'd like to thank my colleagues in the Creative Writing Program at Southern Illinois University, Carbondale: Rodney Jones, Allison Joseph, Judy Jordan, Beth Lordan, Brady Udall, and Jon Tribble.

Oh, let's not forget Ricardo Marcello Vazquez, who will never forget the canolis, and Dave Neis, who will always say, "What do canolis have to do with it?"

*When those went, these went; and when those stood, these stood; and when those were lifted up from the earth, the wheels were lifted up against them: for the spirit of the living creature was in the wheels.*

— EZEKIEL 1:21

# HEFT ON WHEELS

# 1

A truck will hit me.

I'm forty years old, the age of doom coming on and regret setting in, et cetera, but hey, I'm not caught up in all *that*. I'm happy. I'm not overweight anymore. I don't drink anymore or smoke anymore, and, imagine this, I'm not depressed anymore. I'm completely having a great time being healthier now than I've ever been and totally stronger, which is unbelievable sometimes to me. I mean, I expected, when I reached this age, that my athletic life's peak would occur on a Sunday afternoon in January, slamming pitchers of beer and eating peanuts and watching the NFL playoffs _____ with my buddies at the sports bar, but I didn't go that way, I guess, or I didn't *stay* that way.

Instead, a couple of years ago, I spent twenty-five hundred bucks of my professor's salary on a race bicycle and started showing up three nights a week for a fast group road ride here in southern Illinois, at Carbondale Cycle, and three nights a week the group handed me my proverbial fat ass on a platter, which stood to reason. Back then, I smoked a pack a day and drank a case or two of beer a week and did shots of tequila or bourbon or kamikazes or you-name-it regularly at the bar with my graduate students. I weighed, suited up in a skintight XXL cycling jersey and shorts, 255 pounds. Five feet ten inches tall, 255 pounds. I shouldn't have shown up for group ride in that condition. I could have been hurt. Seriously. The group was just too much, too fast, flat-out beating the crap out of me every time. It's a miracle I didn't have a heart attack or a stroke or something trying to keep up.

I kept coming back for more, though, because I needed the crap beaten out of me. That's right. I needed atonement. I'm sure my associates at the bar in those days would agree. And, ah, how atonement comes with the group riding out of Carbondale on Dogwood Road into the mobile-home-littered hills and chip-and-seal roads of the Shawnee National Forest and hammering for forty-five miles, pounding over the hills, working inhumanely hard to spit each other off the back of the draftline and make each other suffer the way dropped cyclists have always suffered, like dogs. Man, back in my heavy days, I'd think if I could stay within *sight* of the group, even for short sections of the ride, I'd be scoring an extra-large moral and metaphorical victory. I *win*, I'd think, just because I'm *participating*. The big unhealthy man rides with the local fit fast road-bike group and gets dropped, the inspiring part being the odd truth: He doesn't get dropped as badly as you'd *think* he'd get dropped. Isn't it terrific the big guy can even stay *close* to those little bike racers?

But metaphor only goes so far in this world. Two hundred fifty-five fat drunken pounds: You ride road bikes with people who are a hundred times as fit and a hundred pounds lighter, they kick your ass. It's that simple.

Two years, twenty thousand miles of training and racing later, I weigh 173 pounds, and my lungs are as clear as my head is free of booze.

Speaking of metaphors, check out this one: If I used to go on group ride at Carbondale Cycle because I needed the crap beaten out of me, these days, I go on group ride because I possess the need and the ability to beat the crap out of others.

Let that be lesson number one.

So this Monday group ride in June, I'm the strongest rider. I'm not bragging or presenting myself as twice the man I really am. It's simply true. I'm the strongest. Another guy in town, my buddy Darren, we train together a lot and race for Team MACK Racing in the Masters 35–45 division and basically ride bikes way more than we should, he's much stronger than me and way more experienced and can and will obliterate me on the road whenever the situation warrants, like when I'm bragging about being the strongest rider on group ride, but shoot, he's not along for the festivities tonight. That means, and I vow to bear this responsibility with maturity and style, I'm the boss.

You can see me there, up front, in all my glory, setting the tempo and the vibe. I'm the guy in the Team MACK racing uniform—red, white, and pale blue—riding the battle-scarred Trek 5200 and wearing the loud red helmet and those stupid football-coach, sports-bar-goer glasses that I know look stupid but are important for me to wear, a small reminder of who I used to be before cycling. You will note, too, that I'm pulling our snaky dozen-rider group-ride phalanx at a comfortable, social, conversational pace, making sure we stay together and keep it mellow and have a positive experience in the early part of the ride, which isn't a corny thing to have, a positive experience.

I don't know why, incidentally, I used to think having a positive experience was somehow saccharine and wrong and inexcusable.

You know? Get over it. Be happy. Chat about this-and-that-type things, the awesome sunny weather, the big century ride coming up this weekend, the two-for-one sale on PowerBars at Kroger's. Have a few yuks. Let out a few not-very-serious groans. Cyclists are just so, so much happier than the drunks are at the bar. Cyclists are always saying *awesome* or *exactly* or *that's cool* or *that's excellent*, always praising each other's feats and encouraging each other to dig deep inside and find the thing that makes us work harder and care more and tune in to the frequency that makes us strong and happy and confident.

We ride east for the Carbondale town line on Dogwood Road, the roadside architecture beside which crumbles, along with the quality of the road surface, from new surgeon's homes to squalor and chickens scratching at the front-yard dirt. This is six in the evening, temperature in the high eighties, a golden slant-light behind us, not much traffic, once in a while a car up or a car back, no wind to speak of, couldn't be a better evening for cycling.

Out a ways, redbud trees and old scrub oaks, fallow fields, beat-up sheds and trailers and, near a long dirt driveway, a handpainted billboard warns of trouble afoot in our souls. The billboard depicts a sad-looking man reading a Bible with a skeleton figure leaning over his shoulder and making his life miserable; flames consume the background, but over the years the sun's faded them into cold white voids in the Old Testament distance. The scripture, from Ezekiel 18:31: "Why will ye die?"

Past the billboard, the road becomes a false flat rising over a series of badly filled potholes and, beyond that, around a rutted corner and down a steep S-curve descent at the bottom of which, what we've all been waiting for, the first sharp climb of the evening, the first attack of the night.

A cyclist at the rear yells *Car Back*, and the *Car Back*

passes from one rider's voice to the next forward, all the way to the front, to me (ain't it cool it's me up front?), and I yell it, too, *Car Back*, to let everybody know I've heard the warning and will heed it. Our bikes make a whizzing noise, a popping noise over the chip-and-seal, tires over the loose pebbles, pebbles pinging the spokes, a loose shifter lever rattling here, a water bottle clattering its cage there, chains clicking through the gears' metal teeth, something low and terrified and heaving within cyclists' lungs. A car back.

It comes by, and cool, we're fine, the driver's one of *us*, a fellow cyclist, Christina, who just got done teaching a Spinning class at Great Shapes Fitness Center for Women. She's heading home, a half-mile from here, at the end of a dirt road called Robin Lane. She's driving a huge 1991 Buick Roadmaster Estate Wagon with a Yakima roof rack on it, the biggest model Yakima makes, big enough to hold *nine* bikes, rods extending a full foot beyond the roof on each side. Christina, she totally understands how to pass a group of cyclists; she gives us *space*. She slows appropriately and swings wide around us, and we're all waving and like hey, Christina. After she's around us and disappearing into the S-curve ahead, we're like she's *great*. She's a really *strong* rider. She's so *awesome*.

Everybody's positive. It's so cool we're this way.

We've got a car back again and voices passing *Car Back* forward, and a Dodge pickup goes by, faster than Christina, wilder, closer to us, but then again, the road's narrowing and getting potholed and nasty with more pebbles and rising dust. A vehicle moving at any speed, under these conditions, could appear to be moving faster than it's actually moving, what with the high-pitched waterfall noise the bikes make in the gravel and the closeness of the trees, but it's okay, the truck's gone around the corner and down the S-turn ahead of the group and way out of sight.

The road seems clear to me, so all right already, I'll throw down the first attack and make it an emphatic one to boot. I get low in the handlebar drops now and slingshot through the corner and yell *clear* and lift out of the saddle and run on the pedals to the crest of the rise, piece of cake to put out this effort, hardly elevates my heart rate to do it. Right here, right now, I'm so aware and so grateful that my life has transformed into this magnificent thing I can do, feels like I'm flying on the road, as if I'll reach the top of the hill and keep rising, like E.T. past the open guts of the moon, twenty miles an hour at the top, accelerating over the blind crest and leaning forward on the bike to dive hard into the descent, passing through twenty-five miles per hour now.

A Dodge Dakota, green in the evening sun, fifty yards ahead of me, pulled to the left shoulder, wrong side of the road, driver's-side door next to a row of mailboxes—looks like the guy in the truck's checking his mail and his brake-lights go off and he pulls forward and I just keep on pedaling and positioning myself to swing in behind him and draft up the next rise, keep the speed up over twenty-five easy, get a head start on spanking everybody over the next mile toward Spillway Road.

He's Robert, construction worker, home from framing in a set of master-bedroom doorways at a new half-million-dollar home at the Shawnee Hills Golf Community. He's thirty-three, a guy who's been, as he'll probably tell you, up and down the block a few times. He doesn't have any mail worth paying attention to, a couple of coupon circulars, nothing, no reason to turn right off Dogwood onto Robin Lane and go inside his house and set the mail on the kitchen table to let his old lady Cindy know he's been there, he's come home and proved he at least cares before cruising over to his friend Tom's trailer and hanging out till ten, but what the hell, he'll drive down to the house first, see if everything's okay. He pops the truck in reverse then forward and Ys into me, I'm like whoa and he's gonna hit me and thwack into his front fender and over the hood and spiraling through the air twenty-five feet, around and around and end over end like a skater doing a double axel with a three-quarter twist toward oblivion. The bike separates from my feet and soars due east down Dogwood, and I fly the direction my life's about to go for a while: south and into the ditch.

I land headfirst. I'll remember that forever: smashing headfirst into the roadside gravel, then the follow-through momentum into my shoulder, then flipping over onto my back, and okay, okay: I'm sitting upright in the weeds, elbows propped comfortably on my inner thighs, hands clasped together as if in prayer, as if God has lifted me off my bike and the obsessive life I've been living on the road and slammed me into the ground, upright, where I'll be in proper position to reflect.

God says, "Feel like praying now?"

I say, "As a matter of fact—"

My left leg is trashed. I know this because I can't seem to move it much or I don't think I should just yet. A lump's already rising in the shin's middle, and blood's emerging from an array of gashes on my inner leg at the knee. A dozen or so tiny grass flies have already settled in on the blood, they pop up off it and sink back in, and I can hear riders unclicking from their pedals around me, the sound of bicycle cleats walking on the road. I can see the truck, the guy in it, bearded guy with a flannel shirt and a feed cap and a ponytail, staring blankly forward into the gravel of Robin Lane.

Robert breaks my heart. He does. I'm man enough, I'm forgiving enough, to admit that. He remembers passing the bikers—must have been fifteen of them—and wham: there's a guy and his bicycle flying past the windshield. Man, where did he *come* from? How'd he get here so *fast?*

Sad, sad story. Robert bought this truck only two weeks ago, brand-new off the lot at Smith Dodge Chrysler Plymouth in Carbondale. In order to buy this truck, he needed to have his Illinois driver's license reinstated after a ten-year suspension. Ten years, the guy hasn't had a driver's license. Gets it back. Gets a new vehicle, and boom, he's colliding with a guy on a bike. Something doesn't seem fair about it.

Robert's not drunk, either, or so Lieutenant McCurdy of the Williamson County Sheriff's Department will tell me the next day, "No smell of alcohol about his person"; neither was Robert's ten-year suspension alcohol-related. Robert's problem is simple, he's a shitty driver. He speeds. He rolls through stop signs. And changes lanes in intersections. And fails to yield at only God knows how many right-of-ways. Ignores the rearview mirror of life. Refuses, consequently, to use directional signals.

He's also freaked out. From nowhere, blammo, the bike flies over the hood. Now there's an angry group of people on bikes surrounding the truck, screaming at him, "Don't go anywhere! Stop! Give us your driver's license!"

It's easy to guess how his brain calculates: hasn't had a driver's license for ten years and he probably just toasted some dried vegetables or is carrying a quantity of dried vegetables—or *something*—and he's checking his mail and minding his own business and turning into his street and whack, there's a guy and his bicycle flying over the truck's hood and smashing headfirst into the ditch. This can only mean one thing: cops. They'll be here in a couple of minutes.

He rolls down his window and says, "I gotta get help." Throws the truck in reverse, doesn't notice he almost runs over two cyclists behind him, Ys back on Dogwood, and gets the hell out of here.

He drives a few miles and ditches his truck on a remote fire lane behind his friend Tom's house, then hitches a ride with Tom back home, where he sneaks in and hides in the bathroom, hearing police banging on his front door every half hour till late in the evening, when Cindy gets home from second shift and persuades him to surrender. He never gives a reason for running away, and the cops never try to nail him down on it. The cops charge him with hit-and-run, an open-and-shut case, and he says wow, he totally freaked, he's sorry.

"I gotta get help," he says, and splits.

That's just so honest it breaks my heart.


Here's an idea so amazingly obvious I can't believe it's never occurred to me before: I've always known a truck's been coming for me.

Used to get up in the morning, hung over and raggedy, and call one of my buddies and say, "Damn, I feel like I got hit by a truck."

Or call in sick to work: "Can't make it today. I feel like I got hit by a truck."

I'd really *be* sick, too. Smoker's hack always, for years, like getting hit by a truck every day.

Or, man, I remember stuff like the smell wafting from my college roommate Jim's Chuck E. Taylors: like getting hit by a truck.

Or reading *Waiting for Godot* or hearing Pink Floyd at the Metrodome in Minneapolis or graduating from college or hearing the news that Frank Zappa died or falling in love with my wife or having children or getting older or giving up cigarettes or giving up booze.

What in life *isn't* like getting hit by a truck?

So in the ditch beyond the intersection of Dogwood Road and Robin Lane, sitting upright, hands folded in prayer, I am not surprised to learn that getting hit by a truck feels exactly like getting hit by a truck.

I will remember my leg smacking the truck's front fender and how, for an instant, my leg feels the smoothness of the truck's finish, then nothing—my brain permanently erases the spectacular twenty-five-foot rotating vault I made through the air—then my helmet crunching into the gravel and me sitting there, praying.

Wham: that fast. I can't make it more complicated than that. Getting hit by a truck *is* getting hit by a truck.

Let that be lesson number two.

But damn, look at this, my bike, my trusty Trek 5200 on which I've ridden myself from fat man on a bike to fit man on a bike, about which I have rhapsodized to my cycling friends lo these three years and twenty thousand miles, it's ruined. It's toast. The truck's impact literally has driven my leg through the carbon-fiber top tube, a material seven times stronger than steel. The frame's busted in half. Both wheels are bent senseless.

My left leg: It's not broken but, considering it smacked into a Dodge Dakota's front fender at thirty miles per hour, probably not race-ready or maybe not even able-to-stand-on-it ready.

My head: bleeding from the right eye and right temple, but the helmet did its job; without it, I'd be either dead or brain-dead.

My shoulder: slightly separated, but my collarbone hasn't broken.

What else? The ribs in my back are bruised bigtime, and the knuckles on my left hand have been ground completely off.

But other than that, yeah, not bad.

Nine days later, early in the morning of July fourth, quarter after six, I'll be riding out Dogwood again. I'll be on a different bike, my Litespeed race bike, which I've never intended to use for tooling around or for training or for rehabbing myself into race form again, but hey, it's the only bike I own. I'm not about to quit cycling because my bike's too *fancy* for riding slow, and that's what I have to do for a while, ride slow.

I'll be taking Dogwood, retracing the fateful route, heading for an easy cruise today with Christina and her husband, Geoff, who live across the road from Robert. They ride a 1971 Schwinn tandem that Geoff's rigged up with disc brakes and a cable system that connects with a child trailer, where they put their baby, Sophia, and lug her over hill and dale for fifty, sometimes seventy-five miles at a crack. The tandem-and-trailer combo makes for an aircraft-carrier-style load, meaning they can't really hammer, at least not uphill, which won't bother me one bit. I'll be a hurting unit, bruised ribs throbbing with each breath, back spasms, left leg stinging at the splinted shin with each pedal stroke, right shoulder killing me, but I'll be used to it and working through it because that's what I do, I ride bikes. I overcome pain. That's what the sport's all about. I understand, as I once heard a football coach say, we need to hurt to heal. It will be almost two months from now till I'm back up to full speed, and even then my full speed won't quite be the same, but I'll get there.

So, on the morning of July fourth, on Dogwood Road, at six-fifteen, Robert will be approaching, going godawful fast, maybe sixty miles an hour on this narrow country road and weaving. I don't think he'll see me, or if he does, I don't think he'll register me as the guy he hit nine days ago. He'll be flying down the road, crazy and reckless, and even though he won't swerve and hit me head-on, I won't take chances. I'll nose my bike into the gravel and off the road.

I'll be fine. Someday I'll stop thinking about it, about trucks and colliding with them, and I'll hold my line confidently in the road again. I'll get over it all right.

But man, it's hard, it's the thwack, the twenty-five feet spiraling through the air that I will never remember, the headfirst hit on the ground, the sitting there with my hands clasped together, the guy in the truck driving away and Gerald appearing, my friend Gerald. I've been training with Gerald every Sunday morning for the last two years; he's in his fifties, is recovering, like me, from alcohol and nicotine addiction, and he can ride a hundred miles on a Sunday morning, in rain or cold or intense heat, and always be in a good mood and put the best possible spin on things.

He's smiling now, in fact. Guy in his fifties, wearing a purple Incredible Hulk cycling jersey. He's found my glasses in the grass, on the opposite side of the road from where I landed. "Not a scratch on them," he says. "They're in perfect condition."

This isn't going to be easy. I'll need help. I'll have to admit I've taken a hard hit and that it will take a long time and a lot of commitment to heal, but right then and there, I get back on my feet, put on my glasses, and resolve to go on.

# 2

Because it's still there. I don't care what anybody might say otherwise. I may not *look* the same as I did a year ago, I may have adopted a different set of *behaviors* since then, but if I'm honest, which is key to recovering from anything, if I tell myself the *truth*, I've got to admit, deep down, way inside the part of me that generates my self-conception, I still believe that I'm the overweight, hard-drinking, chain-smoking person I've been for my entire adult life. I'm serious. That's me. I've only *not* been smoking cigarettes for—what?— thirteen months from the time I quit till the time the truck hits me? That's not a very long time, neither ____

has it been a long time for me since my weight loss, six months, maybe seven or eight. Eleven months, that's how long it's been since I've had any alcohol, definitely not long compared to the years I pounded the stuff down my gullet at the rate of anywhere from two to seven major partying nights a week.

Honestly, ain't no way, this early on in my recovery, am I gonna say I'm cured. Feeling a lot better about myself lately, this is true, and I'm exponentially healthier without question, but one misstep, one little easing up from the disciplined cyclist's lifestyle I'm leading, and there I'll be again, guzzling Rolling Rocks on my patio and smoking Marlboro Mediums and waiting for that extra-large extra-cheese Papa John's pizza to rearrive in my life and bloat me back to championship-caliber beer-drinking form, to 255 pounds of not-so-heavenly joy.

Now, maybe I'm being too hard on myself or maybe the truck has knocked me more senseless than I've been letting on, but I can't help thinking we have some serious misstep potential in this whole truck incident, don't you? I figure I'm slowed up and beat up and terrified and not able to hammer as hard as I've been hammering, not able to ride more than twenty or thirty supereasy, very slow miles at a crack, which is nothing, pathetic compared to the mileage and the intensity I've been putting in.

Man, I've come so far, I'm so worried it's over.

Because it's that simple to give up the discipline, is what I'm saying. I could give up right now. I could go right back where I was, wander back into the bar, grab myself a stool, order a cold one, bam, that simple, and I'd tell myself, *At least a guy ain't gonna get hit by a truck when he's hanging out in the bar, right?*

If I look at a photograph of myself taken even eighteen months ago, maybe while I'm hanging out and partying hearty with my graduate students after some English Department event, eighty-five pounds overweight, relaxing at somebody's picnic table with a beer and a cigarette and a bowl of cheese dip in front of me, if I see that guy in the picture, I certainly don't think that's *not* me. Of course that's me. That's nearly everything I remember about me, prodigious regular drinking since junior year of high school, pack-a-day smoking since my first factory job, at nineteen, and always, no matter what, I've been on the like-to-eat-too-much side of life. Look at any picture of me from grade school, middle school, high school and beyond to the various hard-knocks schools that have occasioned my attendance in the last twenty-two years, you'll see it, you'll see a big boy.

I'm no longer a big boy, true enough, but I remember my missing weight the way a recent amputee might feel a phantom limb where the missing one once was.

My buddy Gerald says it won't do me good to dwell, to beat myself up for things already metabolized into the past, and he's probably right. I shouldn't dwell, but I do anyway. That's the type of person I am, drunk or sober, big or small. Can't do anything about that. Since I was a little boy, I've possessed an excellent memory, particularly for irrelevant technical minutiae that most folks don't care about, which is probably why I've always been destined to become a college professor. That, and I'm good at remembering sets of rules and reciting them over and over in a classroom.

One of my classroom rules, incidentally, is *Learn from your mistakes.*

I used to accept my extra weight as being as much a part of my life as oxygen was to the fire burning my cigarettes, sometimes thirty-five or forty of them a day. And red wine in pint glasses at supper. And pitchers upon pitchers of beer at the bar and kamikaze shots or shots of tequila or bourbon or whatever anybody felt like buying to get the entertainment ramped up and rocking 'n' rolling. Pre-bar. After-bar. Keggers. Margarita madness. Hangovers on Fridays or Wednesdays or Mondays. Hangovers so horrible I needed thirty-ounce chocolate malts to calm my stomach. Or better yet, *blender drinks* to calm my stomach, to quell the hangover hunger that can only be satisfied by potato chips or grilled cheese sandwiches or popcorn or, yes, the macho nachos with the forty-eight-ounce fountain cherry Coke and, along with it, certainly much lying on the couch hung over and watching TV and feeling depressed and obese and unloved and sorry for myself, et cetera.

Another of my classroom rules: *If you do something correctly, study how you did it so you can do it correctly again.*

# HEFT ON WHEELS

I spend a lot of time patting myself on the back and reviewing imaginary game film of me losing weight and giving up drinking and quitting smoking. I try to live in a constant state of self-congratulation, which may sound hopelessly egomaniacal to you, but whatever, dude. I gotta do what I gotta do, all right?

I've achieved results here. I've proved a lot to myself. I've gone out—for real, in the true world, not the world of people bullshitting each other and themselves at the bar—and I've set down a precisely ordered sequence of major changes to make in my life and have executed each one according to plan, and I have succeeded, mostly without a hitch. I haven't always gone about this the proper way, I've taken lots of risks to get the job done, and I probably should have consulted at the very least a physician before undertaking my program and I didn't do that, shame on me. But again, whatever I did has worked, and whatever risks I may have taken, however ill-headed a professional in the field of lifestyle change may say my plan and the manner of execution of it has been, it doesn't matter at this point. I did it. I made the changes. Successfully. That makes *me* the expert. That makes *me* qualified to give advice, even if I'm only giving advice to myself, something I'm going to keep doing because, lately anyway, my advice has been A-OK.

So here's some: *Listen to people who have succeeded.*

**3**

You wanna know my secret? Here goes: I didn't do it to look better or feel better about myself, I did it because I wanted to excel at a sport I've always loved. Sounds too simple, too one-dimensional, sure it does, but it's true.

I can see myself two years ago, in a vision as vivid to me as if I were still there, living through it, when I'm thirty-eight years old and pretending my life occurs inside a Nike commercial, one of those black-and-white computer-generated spots designed to give you an artistic experience that will empower your lardy butt off the couch and into the shoe store. There's heart-stirring orchestral rock music in the background and close-up shots of little kids along a rainy roadway, raising encouraging fists and mouthing something life-affirming.

Go, go, go, I think they're saying. *Allez, allez, allez.*

Fast, fast, they say. *Vite, vite.*

Let's go. *Allons-y.*

And the rain falls in slow motion, and I appear on the screen, naked and soaking wet and suffering heretofore unsuffered extremes on my Trek 5200 carbon-fiber road-racing bike, my face a picture of concentration and determination and triumph.

Thirty-eight years old, five feet ten inches tall, 255 pounds. That expanse you see around middle is my thirty-eight-year stockpile of beer and hamburgers and pizza and nachos and all the other horrible stuff with which I have abused myself over the course of my life, and while Nike is not paying me a blessed dime for saying this, I want you to know that when you see me out there in the countryside going balls-to-the wall on my Trek 5200, hammering at thirty miles per hour down a straightaway, then try to tell me that *my* body is not the *perfect* body for cycling.

You wanna buy some shoes?

Because if you look for the ideal cyclist's body, you *obviously* won't find mine: you'll find Lance Armstrong's body. Like me, Mr. Armstrong stands five feet eleven. Unlike me, Mr. Armstrong is as lean as a pencil, four percent body fat, and has a VO2 max in the gazillion range. He weighs the foods he eats and counts calories to make certain the amount of calories coming *in* matches what his body puts *out*. At peak form, in July, when he's obliterating his rivals on the great climbs of the Tour de France, he weighs roughly 155 pounds. And it is precisely because he weighs 155 pounds that he is able to win. He possesses the power of a much *heavier* cyclist—matter of fact, the 185-pounder he used to be, before he was stricken with cancer—and now he can bring all that power to bear on a frame that's thirty pounds lighter.

In the 2001 Tour, for instance, he crushed Jan Ullrich, his chief rival, principally because he and Jan have equivalent strength in their legs, but Jan weighed in for that Tour at about 170 pounds. Jan Ullrich, champion of Germany, Olympic Time Trial champion, winner of the 1997 Tour de France, one of the greatest cyclists ever, he was too heavy to beat Lance Armstrong. And if Jan Ullrich is too heavy, well, this means I'm the cycling equivalent of a Double Whopper with cheese and supersize fries and an extra-large vanilla shake.

But of course I'm no Jan Ullrich. I'm a lowly recreational rider or, more accurately, a middle-aged guy with a weight problem, lots of enthusiasm, and a fancy race bicycle. In the peak of the summertime, when I'm at my best form, I'm spending fifteen to twenty hours a week in the saddle and riding sometimes in excess of three hundred miles per week, which is nothing to be ashamed of—quite a feat, actually, considering my pack-and-a-half-a-day smoking habit and all the partying I'm doing. Last season, from the first of April to the first of November, I rode a total distance of 5,100 miles. By Lance Armstrong's standards, this is a minuscule effort—what isn't a minuscule effort by Lance's standards?—but compared with the normal person who may from time to time take out a bicycle for a spin, I can be correctly classified as a hammerhead.

On Monday, Wednesday, and Friday evenings, I ride with a group that's based out of Carbondale Cycle, a bike shop here in town. Check us out when we're in front of the place assembling for a ride. We're in the bright cycling jerseys and have the prerequisite superawesome race bikes. The average rider weight: 165 pounds. The average height: five feet eight. The National Football League won't be scouting this bunch anytime soon, which is perfectly fine with them because, in cycling, David will destroy Goliath every time. Guaranteed.

To give you an idea just how much heavier I am than these folks, the closest big guy to me in the group is a fellow who everybody calls Tubby Scott. He's my height and weighs between 205 and 215, depending on how many times he's done the Pizza Hut lunch buffet during the week and in turn how many miles he has ridden. So let's say he's 210 pounds and is as a consequence known as Tubby Scott. What does this mean everybody calls *me?*

I don't believe I want to know.

Carbondale is a college town, the home of Southern Illinois University, and at the beginning of every ride we take a parade route past the bars on the strip, past the frat houses and party houses. Sometimes drunk people cheer at us, which we enjoy, and stupid people sometimes throw water balloons at us, which we hate, but in that first part of the ride, when we're slowly warming up through campus, I feel like I'm part of something special. I'm the big man in the middle of this rolling squadron of muscle, rubber, and titanium. To anyone but the genuine hammerheads I'm riding with, I'm one of the finest cyclists in southern Illinois, and that's awesome to me.

Some of the folks in our peloton are truly great riders, too: accomplished female riders and guys who win weekend road races or place in the top five in the Illinois road-racing championships. Everybody's a hammer. And during the parade warm-up these terrific riders will speak with me about the things cyclists find interesting: "That's an awesome carbon-fiber fork." Or "Have you tried that new double-caffeine PowerGel?" Or "Do you take Cytomax for recovery or Endurox R4?" I love that kind of talk—makes me feel like I'm living within the pages of *Bicycling* magazine.

We're all friends in the peloton. We've shot the breeze on easy days, when everybody's cruising and the pack is just a rolling cocktail party, riders pulling up alongside one another to rehash the high points of last weekend's big ride, discuss who was strong and who drafted off whom. We work hard other days, pushing the pace line, and sometimes, because I'm the widest guy in the pack, I get to drive the train, to be in the lead for a long flat stretch, which is awesome for me but maybe not so for the first five people caught in the rain of sweat I leave in my wake.

My best buddy in our group is a guy from Thailand named Somsak "Saki" Thipkhosithkun. We train together in the winter, riding on our indoor trainers and watching videotapes of—who else?—Lance Armstrong. Saki stands about five feet five, weighs 135 pounds, doesn't smoke, doesn't drink, watches his fat intake, et cetera. When he's at his heaviest and in turn at his cycling saddest, he weighs in at 145. He's the kind of person who wants everyone who rides a bicycle to get the most out of the experience, and this is a good way for him to think because Saki manages Carbondale Cycle. He'll sell you a bike, sure—in fact, he sold me mine, for $2,500—but he wants you to *use* the bike and allow it to transform the way you *live*. As you'd expect, he's quite handy with advice for anybody who trains on bikes. His advice to me is this: *You think too much, Mike. Don't worry about beating the little guys. You ride within yourself, and you'll keep up with the group every time*. I like Saki a lot, and I value his opinion as much as that of anyone I've ever known, but I outweigh the guy by more than a hundred pounds. So I tell him, "Saki, you strap two bags of rock salt on *your* back and go out riding with these animals. Tell me *then* if you don't start thinking too much."

This is what makes me think: After we parade through the Southern Illinois University campus, we always head south. At the south edge of campus is the exact geographic point where the glaciers of the last ice age came to a halt, so the earth is basically as flat as a pool table from Carbondale all the way north to Chicago. But heading south means going up because south of Carbondale lies a labyrinthine configuration of steep hills that constitute the old coal-mining country of southern Illinois. We ride on routes known as Union Hill, or Honker Hill, or the Smiley Face Hill, or Lingle Hill, and the hardest one, which by some miracle doesn't have the word *hill* in its name, is a route called Rocky Comfort, which is actually hillier than all the other *hill* rides put together and no comfort at all.

Lance says he likes to cycle because he likes to suffer. And in this sense, I enter a level of cycling purity unsurpassed by the little people with whom I ride. I get pissed when they zoom up the hills as if it's nothing, but their experience is nowhere near the acute torture mine is. I can outsuffer those runts, and no matter how I gasp and cough and want to puke during a ride, that suffering makes my time on the bike worthwhile.

When the attacks begin—meaning that someone blasts off the front of the pack—we are climbing into these hills, and our peloton changes from a bunched pack of pleasant people chatting about cycling gear to a long string of riders suffering along the road. And at the back of this long string is where I'll be: 255 pounds of sweat and hard breathing and guts churning with Gatorade and PowerGel and the Taco Bell that I know I shouldn't have eaten for lunch. The farther into the long climbs, the farther I drop back, till I'm as much as six hundred yards behind every-body and all alone, with only the roadside flowers and dog-wood trees to see the effort I'm putting forth.

But the diamond in every hill's lining is that if you go up, you'll eventually go down, and when descending, par-ticularly the long straightaway descents of the type we occasionally have in southern Illinois, I am, like Frosty the Snowman, the greatest belly-whomper in the world. The little guys relax on the long descents, to recover and gather their strength for another climb, and this, of course, is the proper way to cycle—ride hard; recover; ride hard; recover—but the long descents are my only chance to catch up, so I click into the biggest gear I can crank and I let it rip. I go flat-out. I maintain speeds of thirty miles per hour, sometimes thirty-five: a 255-pound freight train clos-ing in on the pack. And after a few minutes, when I finally fall in with the group and draft off the little guys and my breath is under control, boom, we're on another climb, and there I am again: six hundred yards behind and keeping company with the dogwoods.

When I was younger and prone to thinking too much, I used to believe Albert Camus's essay "The Myth of Sisy-phus" was the finest assessment of human life ever written. Camus writes about Sisyphus, that poor bastard doomed for eternity to push a rock up a hill, only to have the rock roll back down again. Camus argues that when Sisyphus is walking back down the hill to resume his struggle, he's probably happy because he gets to relax and reflect and check out the scenery. I can't help thinking that if Camus had been a 255-pound cyclist on group ride in Carbondale, Illinois, he would have written that Sisyphus *never* gets to relax. He's got to *hammer* down that hill so he can start pushing his rock again at the same time everybody else does. A big guy on a bicycle never gets to relax.

But that's what makes me happy: struggling. After a couple of hours and forty-five miles, the skies will grow dark, and when the peloton arrives back at Carbondale Cycle, I'll be more or less right there with everybody. I might roll in five or ten minutes behind the great racers, but so what? Saki is right: *You ride within yourself, and you'll keep up with the group every time.* I may never beat these people, hey, but I can sure join them, and that's good enough for me.

So if I'm out there riding with you, and you think you're a badass cyclist, a hammer, a machine, and you're feeling all smug about yourself because you're a few hundred yards ahead of me on that long, long hill, let me tell you, buddy, if I can see you on the road ahead of me, if I'm anywhere close to you, I'm really kicking your ass.

Here's another piece of advice: *Never accept moral victory.*

Because it's not victory, it's ridiculous, it's a lie, nobody wants to be overweight and unhappy and not reaching maximum potential. You're that way, and life itself is kicking your ass, and you know it, and if you don't know it, you're too drunk to know it. Nobody wants to say, with *pride*, hey, I'm eighty-five pounds overweight! Or this, I completely dig smoking *at least* thirty cigarettes every day, and I'm enjoying the heck out of this breathing problem I'm developing. And I absolutely *love* being hung over three, four, five days a week and depressed all the time! And when I ride my bike, something I've wanted to be good at my entire adult life, I am just *so happy* I'm the slowest rider in the group.

No way. Not possible.

But I'm a drunk overweight depressed smoker and am therefore an extremely skilled rationalizer. I can argue this moral-victory stuff till Christmastime, if you'd like.

Listen to this rationalization, a real classic: Besides, it's true, metaphor or not, that I'm far from the worst cyclist in town—not even on group ride am I always the slowest. If I'm riding solo and see another cyclist up the road, I will more often than not be able to run that person down, as they say. I can catch them, I can go faster than them. Maybe that's good enough.

# 4

Quick rule, with compulsory long explanation: *Study your history with the thing that eventually cured you.*

Ah, that would be road cycling. That would be my secret weapon or whatever. And I guess, despite the sloth I've been describing and its attendant general unhealth, I've been riding bikes, with varying levels of fanaticism, for years and years. Not merely riding up and down the block, either, or coasting to the corner store and back; totally getting into it as a major deal in my life. My parents still have the pictures: me at eight years old, in a white T-shirt and jeans and PF Flyers, mounted on my first ____ bike, a twenty-inch Schwinn Typhoon; or, when I'm in sixth grade, in a yellow shirt, gripping the handlebar drops and hammering down the street on my fancy yellow twenty-four-inch Schwinn Varsity ten-speed; or, in high school, on my full-size twenty-seven-inch Schwinn Continental, wild-eyed and happy.

Any picture of me on a bike, I've got those same eyes, like this is where I belong, boy and machine, an open road of hard-charging good times ahead of me. That's just the way it is, I've always loved riding bikes and have always loved going a little longer and a little harder and all that romantic stuff, rolling for destinations that seem a bit too far away, too high up, a bit too difficult. It's the getting-there I've always thought is cool about cycling, the adventure of it, not to mention I flat-out love the feeling of rolling down the road, the wind, the view, every part of the experience, even the it-hurts part. I've owned lots of different bikes, too, and loved every one of them in a tremendously profound and passionate way, which is to say I have stared at my bikes with longing and desperation and jealousy when I'm not riding them or not cleaning their chains or rubbing wax into their downtubes late in the evening, et cetera.

It's okay. My wife knows all about it.

My best period of cycling, because that's what it was, a *period*, one I'm ashamed to say didn't last, was when I was twenty-four years old and working second shift as a machine technician, a mechanic, at a plastics factory in Eau Claire, Wisconsin, commuting on a powder-blue Miyata 512 six miles each way, generally six days a week, as well as getting up in the morning five or six days a week and riding thirty or forty or fifty or even a hundred miles. Add it up, that's easily 250 miles a week. That's some fairly serious mileage, hours and hours in the saddle. You have to be a huge fanatic to put in that kind of time on a bike. So there you go, twenty-four years old, I had fanaticism, I had the cure available right then.

I bought my Miyata from a really cool hippie dude named Dave, who owned The Bike Doctor in Eau Claire. He was the type of person you want to buy a bike from. Not just a shop owner—sort of like the hair-replacement commercial goes—but a client, a guy totally into bikes in a way that had nothing to do with business, it was love for Dave, it was life. The guy rode *all* the time, almost never drove his car except maybe to an out-of-town race on a weekend or, in the winter, off somewhere to go cross-country skiing. When I'd go down to his shop and listen to him talking about riding long loops on the weekends or going on hard training rides, people really kicking it up out there, really pasting each other and shaking and baking and in general romping and stomping and having a great time on the road, I'd be like yeah, this guy is on to something very cool.

One day I was cycling to work and met up with Dave and rode along with him for a few miles. I kept the pace I'd normally set to work, flat road, twenty-two miles per hour, steady eddie, easy McGreasy, didn't want to get there too soon but then again didn't want anybody to see me riding slow and looking *weak*. I guess Dave was impressed, in any case, and mind you I absolutely respected the guy and looked up to him; he told me, "I know people who could teach you to ride thirty miles per hour."

I've never forgotten that moment, one of those I-have-an-untapped-potential moments. The guy thought I was fast, that was *cool*. And I've never forgotten my strength at the time and my stamina: working on industrial machinery fifty and sixty hours a week, extremely physical labor; riding as hard as I could 250 miles a week; drinking at the bar two or three nights a week; never sleeping more than five hours a night; and I could keep running myself like this for weeks and weeks and never get wound-down or burnt-out or overtired.

Fourteen years ago. Wow, I was an animal, dude.

Gerald tells me not to beat myself up. But man. If only I had focused my energies on the bike back then.

A hard winter blew in, as it inevitably will in west central Wisconsin, and the weather became too cold and too miserable for cycling and in turn looked favorable for other sports, indoor sports like playing dice at the bar or playing pool or throwing darts or, my strongest event at the bar, sitting on a stool for three to five hours and plying the ancient art of drunken conversation. I did well at the bar, really improved on all aspects of my game there. By the time the next summer came along, I opted to forgo cycling and instead concentrate completely on tavern sports, where I felt I possessed greater potential than on the road.

For the next six years I didn't ride much bike. Once in a while I'd put some air in the tires and go for a spin but never with any consistency. I was too busy underachieving at work and underachieving in the college classes I took, which is extra-pathetic because I was taking underachiever-style classes in the first place: European Novel, Creative Writing, Studies in Poetry, Modern Drama, and so forth. I believe, in any event, that I spent more time in the bar discussing maybe getting around to doing something productive someday than I actually spent doing anything. I needed lots of relaxing, is what I figured, and of course much discussion. That's where learning takes place, right? In discussion?

I'm inspired to sing:

O to be a man in his twenties, working in a factory and dreaming of becoming a writer. To sit down and talk, really *talk* about these things, whatever they are. That's it! Go to the bar and *sit* and *talk* and become somebody!

I even studied, for hours, not so I'd do better in school but so I could be a better conversationalist at the bar. For example, I read, or tried to read, a bunch of epic novels and proceeded to discourse at great length on them at the bar, probably in the process proving to my fellow conversationalists that I didn't understand those novels one bit, but that's nothing I'm embarrassed about; you're not supposed to understand epic novels, nor are you really supposed to say anything intelligent in a bar.

When I was thirty, I don't know why, but I got lucky, and I got accepted into graduate school—into the creative writing program at Minnesota State University at Mankato—and awarded a teaching assistantship and all that good stuff. This was a great break for me, and I took it seriously and became fanatic about working hard on my writing and really being intense about everything having to do with school. Two years, that's how long I was there, best two years of my life. No lie.

I became friends with a guy from my writing classes, a Vietnam vet named Bob, who wasn't really a student in the graduate program but a guy from the community, a guy who worked maintenance at the phone company and who happened to write better than any of the students in the graduate program. I respected him a lot and learned a lot from him; to this day I count him as the best friend I've ever had.

One of the things I learned from Bob: *A person can be happy and have a good time without being drunk.*

He had been in recovery from alcohol for eight years and had picked up tennis to replace his hours at the bar,

not to mention he picked up tennis because he loved playing tennis, which stood to reason because the man could
play some awesome tennis. He could kick the crap out of
guys half his age. I assume, back in his day, with his
strength and quickness and endurance, he had been a phenomenal competitor at the bar.

Anyway, I owned a mountain bike and he owned a
mountain bike, and what the hell, we started riding
together regularly on a flat converted railroad bed called
the Sacatah Trail. We'd ride out twelve miles to Eagle Lake
and sit on a picnic table overlooking a southern Minnesota
slough with white pelicans flying in circles above the reeds,
and we'd smoke a few cigarettes (well, nothing's perfect)
and shoot the breeze, talk about books and writing and
have a few yuks at the expense of the dipsticks we had to
put up with in our writing classes, then we'd ride the twelve
miles back into town. Never have had a better friend than
Bob. Never have had better times than riding bikes on the
Sacatah Trail with Bob.

He didn't drink, and I got to thinking sometimes
maybe I shouldn't, either, but the pull to party was too
strong. I was single and in graduate school in Creative
Writing, which, in case you didn't know, is one of the
drinkingest types of graduate programs a person can under-
take. All those aspiring poets and novelists and all their
aspirations and torments and needs to act them out in front
of others—what do you expect? Think they're gonna stay
home and *study*?

One time, Bob and I rode the entire Sacatah Trail from Mankato to Faribault and back, on gravel, forty miles there and forty miles back into a fierce headwind, and to celebrate this, later in the evening I invited a few of my derelict friends over to slam a few cases of Rolling Rock and a bottle of George Dickel and, like, didn't I deserve to get drunk after riding a hard eighty miles out there on the plains of southern central Minnesota? Next morning, when I was nearly dead from the combination of hangover and bike-tiredness, I went to work at my part-time job delivering laundry for a nursing home. Drove my laundry van past the tennis courts, nauseated and disoriented and desperate to get off work and go back to bed, and there was Bob, charging the net and smacking the ball back in his opponent's face and taking the point. He felt great, I felt like crap. I thought, Bob might be on to something here.

Maybe I was drinking too much, but I was functioning in life. I kept my teaching assistantship and worked every weekend at the nursing home and earned straight A's through my master's degree course of study. Somewhere in there, I won a writing contest and after that I got accepted into the creative writing program at the University of Florida, proof to me I had no reason to say to myself, Magnuson, you're screwing up. You'd better stop drinking and take your life seriously.

See, in my twenties, partying was something that got me in trouble because I was young and stupid and all that;

now in my early thirties, in my thinking, because why would I have thought otherwise?, partying was furthering the advancement of my career. It was helping me to be a fun and amusing person with whom to argue about Sylvia Plath and John Milton and Form and Theory of the English Sentence and other learned topics into the wee hours of the morning.

And in Mankato I met the woman who would become my wife, and we got married in one of those entertaining ceremonies where not too many people show up and a violinist plays Frank Zappa's "Idiot Bastard Son" while the wedding-party members saunter up the aisle and take their places for the main event and, later in the evening, the bride's and groom's friends kidnap them and take them to the Square Deal Bar in downtown Mankato and buy them shots.

A great wedding, all in all. Wish you were there.

And it came to pass that I moved to Florida, where all of a sudden the partying was even better and more magnificent than ever.

By the way, check out Gainesville sometime. Amazing.

I'd say, if you're looking for a grade-A partying college town, Gainesville should be tops on your list. Great bars. Great restaurants. Lots of opportunities to party outdoors, all year round. From Gainesville, too, you can literally, as the great Gainesville resident Harry Crews has pointed out, drive an hour to catch the sunrise over the Atlantic Ocean and, later in the day, be hanging out in Cedar Key drinking beer and waiting for the sun to set over the Gulf of Mexico.

I loved it in Gainesville.

Every time I went for a bike ride, though, I seemed to get a flat tire or have a mechanical problem or get rained on (you wouldn't believe how much it rains in Florida), and pretty soon I was blowing off riding more and more and sitting on my butt doing my homework or hanging out at a bar called the Salty Dog and somehow, in the full hot Florida summer of 1996, at the same time as the Olympic Games, I contracted the Chinese intestinal flu or whatever it was and had diarrhea for ten days at least; when I tipped the scales at the doctor's office, after not having eaten *anything* for more than a week, I weighed 245 pounds. Add food and water: we were easily looking at a weight as high as 260. The thing is, I saw that 245, and I was thrilled. I said to my wife, "I'm finally losing weight."

I had never been heavier or more out of shape or more in need of fresh air, clean living, and plenty of exercise, which was something my wife, who knows about health—because she's a nurse, for one thing, and because she's never been an overweight hardcore boozer like me—she could no doubt recognize this in me, but was too kind to dress me down for it. What she did do was arrange for us to get a membership to the greatest gym in America, the Gainesville Health and Fitness Center, which happened to be a mile or so from our house. This gym, I'm telling you: incredible. It's the size of, say, a Super Wal-Mart but twice as big, a double-decker one with two stories. There's day care, no extra charge, seven days a week, which mattered at this point because my wife and I had ourselves a little girl.

And as far as equipment, name it, it's there, and in vast quantities. Rows and rows of treadmills and stairmasters and elliptical trainers and TVs, of course, to keep you from becoming bored. And ten rows of Cybex weightlifting machines; when you go through "the line," as they call it, an employee wearing either a tie or a skirt takes your card that's got your machine settings on it, and then the employee goes down the line and sets up everything for you and writes down your numbers for you when you move through. Upstairs, free weights and rooms for aerobics classes and yoga and kickboxing and more treadmills and elliptical trainers and sit-up machines and on and on and on.

Great gym. I defy you to find one that's better.

But I hated it. I didn't want to walk on a treadmill and watch TV! I mean, I could stay at home and walk laps around my yard and have the same experience. And I didn't want to do step aerobics or start lifting weights or whatever else because why would I? I'm not saying those are bad things to do, I'm just saying they don't happen to trip my trigger. No matter how hard I try, I can't muster any passion for walking on a treadmill.

I'm going to tell my students this today, even if life generally makes it an impossible rule to follow: *Don't do things if you're not passionate about them.*

The truth: *You have to lower your standards, accept what's available to you, and become passionate about what's available to you.*

Then the gym rebuilt an aerobics room to accommodate studio cycling, Cycle Reebok, essentially exactly like Spinning but with a different brand of stationary bikes. They put in thirty-two of these bikes arranged in a row of semi-circles, facing a raised platform where the instructor would sit on her bike and call out routines, ups and downs and harder-harder-harders, all to the tempo of Van Halen or Whitesnake or the Bangles or whatever butt-stomping tempo-riding music the instructor had selected. You know *me*, I saw all those cool-looking black bikes and heard those tunes thudding, and I was like, What's going on in *there?*

Killer stuff. I'm telling you.

My wife and I started going to the classes, a nice thing for a couple to do, drop the baby off in the gym's day care, suit up, stretch out, blast through a Cycle Reebok session, and get a fantastic workout in the process. Do this five-six days a week for a few months, make it a lifestyle, and what do you get? Fit.

And they had great instructors for the classes, a sign of a top-of-the-line gym right there, knowledgeable instructors, people committed to helping folks in the class improve and have a positive experience every single time they work.

A teacher like this says *Do it*. And the students do it. Should be a rule in *that*, don't you think?

# HEFT ON WHEELS

After a few months I started to get in fairly decent condition, at least in the Cycle Reebok sense. I was doing a class sometimes three times in a day, sometimes three times in a row, and it might be that during this period I embodied the Fit or Fat thing that Covert Bailey made famous way back when. I certainly was not a skinny person—230 pounds, lean and mean for me but, you know, high in the body-fat-percentage department—but I wasn't out of shape by any stretch, with the exception that I still smoked in excess of a pack of cigarettes a day and still got drunk at least twice a week.

Not a few mellow beers, either. I'm talking epic close-the-bar-and-then-drink-after-bar hammering, endurance drinking of the highest order, but it didn't matter much anymore, I didn't think. I could handle it. I literally had worked out a schedule for drinking so that I would drink hard and get blitzed on the universal collegiate drinking night, Thursday, then, on Friday afternoon, I would attend Cycle Reebok, hung over as hell, and sweat out the toxins and purify and attend cycling class again on Saturday morning and purify more so I would be fully charged and ready, on Saturday night, to hang out on my deck with two coolers packed with Corona and ice and get blasted to outer space. Oh, and then I'd take Sunday off Cycle Reebok for sleep purposes. In this way, I only had to do Cycle Reebok with a hangover one day a week. Genius plan, no?

I had no reason to believe otherwise.

At the end of my third year in Gainesville, I had gotten progressively more fit, had dropped to 220, was having fun with all my cool friends, was doing fine with my career— published a couple of novels, got to hot-dog around the country a bit in promotional support of them—and I had stayed on at the university after getting my degree; they hired me to teach for a year as a Visiting Assistant Professor, in the furtherance of which I presided over a series of crazy freeform courses with no syllabus and pitchers of beer after every class at the Salty Dog with my students, many of whom had been my fellow students only the year before.

So, sure, I couldn't stay at the University of Florida forever and self-actualize with drinking and studio cycling and believing the party ain't never gonna end. They cut me loose after my one-year gig, maybe exactly because I made no secret of going to the bar and partying hearty with my students or maybe because the university had standards and it was best for the writing program if its graduates went forth in the world and got jobs at other institutions, but in any case I was thirty-four, with a wife and a child, and I was out of a job, at least a teaching job, and I moved from Florida back to my hometown of Menomonee Falls, Wisconsin, to get away from it all.

My students often disagree with this rule, but I believe it's a good rule: *Don't move back to your hometown, especially if you've been gone from it for a long time.*

I had a contract to write a book, which should have

been a marvelous opportunity, a joy, a delight, an occasion to work hard all day and crank out the pages and get serious about making my living as a professional writer, that of course being the pinnacle of achievement, if you happen to be a writer, being able to make a living at it.

My wife and I moved into a townhouse three blocks from the home where I grew up. She got a job at the VA hospital in Milwaukee, about a half hour's drive away, and I set up my office in the laundry room, a tiny cinderblock room in the basement with no windows and low ceilings; in it were the washer and dryer and a utility sink and the furnace and the water softener, and look, look what happened to my life because of that basement:

In the morning I would get up at six with my daughter, Anne, who was two now, and I would fix her something to eat and get her ready for day care and drop her off and lose myself in the fog of my own devices.

My desk in that laundry room. A bare forty-watt bulb over my shoulder. My computer on. A big smoke-eater fan to the left of the keyboard, never turned the smoke-eater off, a constant white noise, and I was smoking constantly, easily two packs a day, more than that some days.

Mornings I would sit there for three hours, maybe four, sometimes typing, mostly not typing, mostly smoking and drinking coffee and reading and rereading the two pages I had managed to write in the last month and deciding, correctly, that they were bad and it was too much effort to go on.

Afternoons, for fresh air, I would sit upstairs and read long books of military history or drive aimlessly around the countryside of my youth, smoking cigarettes and wishing I'd have been happy way back when and that I were happy now. At four, I would pick up my daughter from day care and take her to the grocery store where, just about every night, I would buy ingredients for a large supper and accompany the cooking and the eating with pint glasses of wine. I went through magnums and magnums of wine every week.

Most nights after supper, I would sit in the living room and drink coffee and watch my daughter play or watch reruns of *Homicide: Life on the Streets* till she went to bed and my wife went to bed, and I would return to my desk in the laundry room and smoke more cigarettes and usually make a quart of margarita in a large plastic cup, and I wouldn't work on my book. I would go online and type my name into search engines and see what would come up, same old thing every night, not much.

Occasionally, because this was my hometown, I would hang around with old friends—only had a couple, really—and we'd drink too much and try to figure out why we used to hang around together twenty years ago. We obviously couldn't figure it out because we didn't seem to hang around very much now.

One guy I knew, me and him used to be elite-level drinkers, years back, in 1981, when we worked together at a machine shop for a few months. We used to get off work at four-thirty and do double-bubble at the Fall Inn till seven, vodka gimlets for him, gin gimlets for me, six nights a week, then we'd wander over to a dive called The Old Lamp and get hammered some more over there, where we both were running tabs; that's how regular we were. He was a really big guy back then, in 1981, six feet two and easily 275 pounds, but when I returned, in 1998, he had become a *huge* person. Maybe 350 pounds, maybe pushing on toward 400. And I would say he exhibited characteristics of being a late-stage-alcoholic type of drunk, a guy slurping down a quart of bourbon every evening after work, having blackouts most every night, the kind of drinker who appears to be a regular person when you first see him, at happy hour, when he's not bombed yet and is friendly and speaking intelligently and succinctly, but after so many drinks, God throws the switch on him, or a switch goes off inside him, and the guy instantly does a Jekyll into a Hyde, becomes mean and loud and slurring and irrational and repetitive and not really a person at all.

He was the best friend I had, and I only saw him once a month.

Feel sorry for me?

I certainly did. I got so bummed during the winter that I didn't bother applying for a teaching job, something that would have gotten me out of the basement and reconnected me with the university scene, where I could hang out again with dozens of vital and alive and passionate and engaged people and maybe not be so bummed out anymore.

One day I took out the bathroom scale and stood naked on it and weighed 275 pounds and felt so awful I loaded up my .22 rifle and held it for several hours, smoking cigarettes, listening to the smoke-eater grinding my life into pieces.

But spring finally came, and I fixed up my old mountain bike.

I keep wanting to offer evidence. I want to say Look at *this*. Look at how I *knew* how to cure myself the whole time!

For more than twenty years I lived in serious up-and-down cycles, the downs being *exceptionally down*, nearly killing-me downs, they were so bad. Twenty years at least. That's an awful long time to know how to make yourself feel better and never do anything about it.

But there it was, I got back on my bike.

This was in the middle of March, with high temperatures in the low forties, but I rode six days a week, taking it easy at first, riding on the Bugline trail, a converted-to-trail railroad bed that runs from Menomonee Falls west through Lannon and Sussex, old dusty limestone-quarry towns, a dozen miles in a ride, fifteen miles, twenty, working my way up to epic thirty-mile rides that took three hours and left me totally toasted, too exhausted to have a beer, if you'd believe that. I would ride in the rain and in the cold and into the wind and in the sun, my God, how great the sun felt on the soul. How great water tasted again. How I started to feel like a happy person again.

My career picked up, too. By some miracle, my alma mater, University of Wisconsin at Eau Claire, had a temporary teaching job open, teaching English composition, being useful, helping people, making a little money. Needless to say, I jumped at that. I packed up the family, moved north to Eau Claire, and didn't screw up. I showed for work on time, never called in sick, never shirked my duties. I kept riding my bike outside till the weather got nasty, and when it did, I had the ambition to check out Spinning classes at the university, attended them all winter, five days a week. I got serious about getting a permanent job, too, and actually got one, at Southern Illinois University at Carbondale, where I am today and will probably be till I die.

But let's not get too carried away. I was still drinking and smoking and so on. I don't have to keep saying it any longer, do I? I mean, the pattern is so, so predictable that way. Everybody's is.

# 5

 $O$h, I almost forgot. This is one of the hugest of the huge rules: *Your bad habits will catch up to you.*

Drinking, and any experienced heavy drinker will tell you this, it's an endurance sport. It demands incredible stamina and commitment and deep reserves of energy and the will to stay out there on the course well past the time the weaker competitors have dropped out and gone to sleep. Because of the intense demands made on the body and the mind, the farther along drinking's strongest players get in their careers, the more they begin fraying at the edges of performance. They get more tired than they ____

used to, more forgetful, more irritable, less caring, less able to give a damn, or they begin having equipment failures, physical problems, financial problems, problems associating with people not involved in the sport, which becomes an individual sport by and by: the individual and the booze and the long hazy slog toward the finish line.

An associated rule: *Go ahead and look around at the competition.*

I might have been lucky, in fact, that I was traveling through my past, moving first back to my hometown and then back to my alma mater, because I could drink again with old drinking buddies and compare how they seemed now with how they used to behave and to appear to me long ago.

My buddy in Menomonee Falls, he obviously needed treatment.

In Eau Claire I had a buddy, old buddy, we kept in touch while I was gone doing my thing and he'd been staying put doing his thing, drinking double bourbons every afternoon and into the evening for the ten years since I moved away. Used to be, years ago, the guy was the proverbial sharpest tack in the bar, funny, outrageous, knew a little bit about everything, great storyteller, passionate conversationalist, and on and on. An incredibly interesting person. But I don't know how else to say it: The booze had clearly beaten him down, at least that's the way he appeared to me at the bar, thin and vague and forgetful and always exhausted or distracted or muttering the same story over and over again about, say, that gal he used to know way back or about his current mistress, wow, she can really put 'em away, really sit at the bar for hours and always have something interesting to talk about.

Maybe the booze hadn't beaten him down. Maybe ten years is just a long time, and people age a lot more in ten years than I had expected, but I'd see the guy at the bar and talk with him and often get angry with him—could have been over anything but always over *something*, always we bickered at the bar—and if I'd see him the next day, he would *never* remember any hostilities that might have been exchanged between us. He'd hardly even remember having seen me at all. Yeah, maybe it wasn't the booze that changed him, but I couldn't help taking note of the changes in him and saying to myself, *Keep it up for another ten years, Mike, this is going to happen to you.*

When I moved to Carbondale, a small college town— need I say more? I mean, is there anything else to do in a small college town *but* get drunk? I made no secret of my thirst for tavern-style misbehavior, matter of fact, when I interviewed for the job here. I promoted it as a job asset even, and therefore totally got smashed, all three nights I was here on interview, at a smoky basement bar called the Cellar. I did shots with the graduate students and slammed brews with them, had much excellent drunken laughter and hoo-ha, and wasn't I the perfect fellow to come to town and hang out in the bar for a few years with the grad students and discuss *craft*?

My first fall here, I taught a large graduate writing seminar on Wednesday nights, and because of a strange extra-long-fall-semester way they schedule classes at Southern Illinois University, it turned out we had seventeen class meetings, and after every single class I went out with the students and did some of the most supremely professional drinking I'd ever done in my life, eight p.m. till two a.m. at the Cellar, then almost invariably over to somebody's house to hammer on till sometimes five in the morning. I honest to God was drinking on an Olympic level with my students, who, in turn, were doing horribly with their schoolwork because they were too drunk to know the difference between authentic good work and talking about good work at the bar. Implicit in this, of course, is that I didn't know the difference, either.

Reminds me, there was somebody teaching here that year on a one-year temporary gig, kind of like the gig I'd had in Eau Claire the year before. He was your classic mildly famous unknown writer on whose short stories an occasional country-and-western song has been based. A literary genius, as they say in the bar. A scholar. Used to be a bigshot, but he was a go-to-the-bar-at-nine-in-the-morning guy now. I'd see him a bit before noon, up at school, when he was getting ready to teach, and he'd be wobbly and letting off that supersour stink of a person who's maintained a .25 blood-alcohol level for several weeks. Drunk twenty-four-seven. And I hung out with him and laughed and talked smack with him *all the time*. We were grand friends. Dig what I'm saying?

You should have seen me down there at the Cellar with my literary genius buddy and the graduate students. We should have gotten it on film, it was so stupendous. Amazing stuff. By nine o'clock we'd have six or eight people sitting around a table (all smokers, of course) and two pitchers of beer going at all times, sometimes three or four or five pitchers, depending on who all showed up as the night wore on. After the first hour of beer blitz, then for sure I'd buy a round of shots for everybody at the table, which for sure would guarantee that in a while somebody *else* would buy a round of shots and so on down the line till, after a couple of hours, each member of our literary crew had quaffed roughly ten pints of beer and five or so shots of kamikaze or whatever, and wow, it's only midnight, bar doesn't close till *two!*

I'm not saying this wasn't *fun*, but, as we often happily said to each other in the university hallways the next day, we were getting *way* out of hand.

Ha! That reminds me of another guy in Carbondale, husband of one of my colleagues, guy in his fifties, guy with no job, he drank something milky-looking with vodka in it every afternoon, probably straight vodka with a splash of 50/50, but I knew better than to take a sip, which ought to be a rule right there: *Never drink the drink the drunk drinks*. He drained numerous large glasses of this drink every night and of course, with dinner, enjoyed several glasses of wine and then had more drinks after that, and he always, always reached that point in drinking when his inner switch would flip and he'd get incredibly loud and argumentative and flat-out unable to understand what anyone might have to say about anything. Everybody was wrong and stupid and misguided, and he would scream and holler and throw all manner of tantrums till he proved to his satisfaction that he was in the right.

One time I went to the Cellar with him, and a kid came near him and took his picture with a digital camera, and he became instantly furious, jumped up from his stool, tore the camera from the kid's hand, slammed it to the ground, and stomped it to bits with his heel.

Lovely.

He basically did stuff like this (still does) several times a week.

My assessment: That guy's a drunken idiot.

I don't know about you, but I don't want to be a drunken idiot.

But there it was. I was drinking more than ever and getting more argumentative with people and feeling tired and forgetting people's names and repeating myself, telling the same stories over and over, and the only positive thing in all this was that I knew I was getting out of hand. I knew I had a drinking problem and eventually, if I didn't die first, I'd have to do something about it.

# 6

In the middle of April, in 2002, on a blustery Wednesday night, mounted on my Trek 5200, I'm on the way from my house to Carbondale Cycle, to group ride. I'll be turning thirty-nine in a couple of weeks. I weigh 255 pounds. I'm not hung over, though I will be for sure on Friday because I teach night class on Thursday night. I've been hung over a lot lately. I'm run-down and irritable and behind on my work at school and behind on lots of projects I've got going on. Everything, even my bike, feels like it's pointed in the wrong direction, but I will always believe that my whole life has lined up to create this moment, this ____

evening's ride, because after tonight's ride, I will have found the motivation to turn myself around.

That book I was hating to write in Menomonee Falls, I've finally finished it and it's been published, basically to no acclaim, which is okay with me. What's acclaim going to do for me? Make me leaner and happier and a better cyclist? I don't think so. But as a consequence of my no-acclaim book, I've been lucky enough to publish in *Gentleman's Quarterly* an essay on doing what I'm doing this instant, riding my bike, on how funny and sad it is that I have a hard time keeping up on the hill climbs with the skinny, lightweight bike racers here in Carbondale. The essay touches on some other things, too—friendship, self-acceptance, Albert Camus—and it might be heart-wrenching or inspiring or any number of things, but nobody will ever know; nobody bothers to read the essay because of some artwork the editors decided to include with it.

Right there on the first page of my essay, on page 80 of the May 2002 issue of *GQ*, is a five-inch-square color photograph of me, in side view, naked and wet and 255 pounds, mounted on a race bicycle. The picture is outrageous and funny, especially if you're not me. Everybody I know has seen it, you've seen it, it's reprinted on the jacket of this very book you're reading, and you smiled when you first saw it, you were amused, I know you were.

Just look at it: the naked grayish-green-skinned fat man straining into a high wind and a driving rain, near nightfall, past a suburban home that no doubt represents an appropriately modest hearth and a life devoted to doing the best one can and not letting one's limitations stand in the way of self-fulfillment.

Makes you kind of sick, now that you know me, doesn't it?

Anyway, the following advice is for only the toughest of you out there: *Get naked in a national magazine sometime.*

Go ahead and try it. And if you want to feel the maximum effect of the experience, be one of those people who's too ashamed of your lousy body even to take your shirt off at the beach, a remote beach, where no one else is there to see you shirtless in the first place. Then, when your naked picture appears in a magazine with a circulation of 300,000, see if you don't find the motivation to make a few significant lifestyle changes.

This evening's weather is way worse than blustery: gusting winds, and the sky is roiling with grayish-green clouds, the type of clouds that here in the lower Midwest cause people to contemplate Munchkins and yellow brick roads and all those terrifying things that lurk somewhere over the rainbow, where life in the trailer park is grim, and supper, if there's supper at all, is likely to be Hamburger Helper seasoned with cigarette smoke and alcoholism and unruly children and despair.

A sane person wouldn't go out biking on an evening

like this. But *not* biking, just now, not *exercising*, that's simply out of the question. Weather looks bad? So what. I'm riding. At least 300,000 people know that I am a fat piece of crap. I am *not* taking the night *off*.

But I guess I've got no reason to feel special. I'm heading out to ride in a storm this evening for my own reasons; the rest of the crew's heading out for theirs. I will not be riding alone. Looks to me that the usual group-ride suspects are present and accounted for when I get to the Carbondale Cycle parking lot, all my 150-pound buddies.

A real cyclist—this is what resolve will teach you—will ride in any weather; we are all motivated and dedicated people.

So with nary an eyeball turned to the horrible sky, we roll out of the parking lot and spin out of town, this evening on a route called Lakes, which isn't the hilliest ride in the group's repertoire, but it's got its share of doozies, the first of these being a sloping upgrade known as Honker Hill, whereon I've never ridden with the group without getting spit off the back like a bad memory.

Which is precisely what happens. I can see the group on the road ahead of me, maybe five hundred yards up Honker Hill, and usually from this distance back they appear like miniature draft animals straining under their burdens, pumping at the pedals and lifting out of the saddle to keep up with each other, but just now, in the wind and in the piercing lightning flashes, I see arms raised and gesturing, some kind of intense conversation going on, and the group slows down.

I keep pedaling along, grinding, sucking it up and riding within myself the way Saki has taught me, and I don't think much of it till I notice one of the fastest guys in the group, a racer named Darren, dropping back from the group to fetch me, which means he'll let me catch up with him, and he'll use his draft to pull me forward to the group.

When we're together, he says, "You *got* to keep up, man. You can't be alone back here in this weather."

He puts the hammer down then, and I try holding on to his back wheel but can't really, not going uphill. And he drops back again, and yells at me. "Get on my wheel, and stay there!" And he pulls me forward for a hundred yards again, and I drop back again. He slows down. And pulls me forward. I try saying, "I've been really busy lately—" But Darren refuses to hear that. "Don't talk," he says. "Pedal."

Finally, after a few hard minutes, we catch the group, which has been slowed all this time waiting, and the winds nearly are blowing people off their bikes, and the lightning is groping across the sky, and the thunder is rolling and beating into the countryside's desolation, and Darren gets into an argument with the hammers who've been waiting.

"We gotta ride *together*," Darren's yelling. "We can't leave people behind in a storm like this."

One of the hammers says, "That guy's too slow to be riding with us in the first place."

I love cycling, that whooshing sound in your ears, that feeling on a descent like flying a sailplane, the afternoons in the countryside with the roadside flowers pink and purple and red and blurring by, the beauty of the road, the goodness of riding on it, the freedom, the confidence. I read about cycling constantly, stare at bike catalogs for hours on end. I follow professional bike racing on the Internet. Cycling is my favorite thing in the world, and there you go: I'm too slow.

Or worse, I'm the idiot in that picture, that naked guy on a bike who, for all anybody but me would know, has merely written an essay about cycling as a goof to make a couple of bucks and then has posed in that stupid picture as a publicity stunt, but it's just not true. You know me. You know cycling's not a joke to me. I wouldn't have been riding for as many years as I have, if I thought it was a stupid thing to do.

Think about this: Salesmen will often bandy about the idea that "you can't sell something that isn't already selling." Or "you can't move something that isn't already moving." Which I think is a close relative of "you can't get a job unless you've already had a job." When I was younger, I could never understand that. I mean, how's a person supposed to get a job in the first place if you need to *have had* a job to *get* a job? But tonight I must have finally become older and wiser, because I can see that I've already taken the most important step in making progress: I'm already riding my bicycle. I'm already moving. All I've needed to decide all these years is what I'm moving *for*.

Right here and now, friends, on this stormy evening outside of Carbondale, Illinois, I know I need to prove something out of this. Cycling's not a joke. I'm not a joke. I don't want to be a figure of fun. I'm not a fat guy on a bike. I'm a real cyclist, and I'm hereafter going to do everything in my power to achieve my fullest potential on the bike, which may not mean that I win races or anything but certainly that I can keep up on a simple little thing like Wednesday-night group ride in a thunderstorm.

To get this done, no way around it, I've got to change my lifestyle completely. I've got to quit smoking and quit drinking and lose weight and start treating my body like an engine, like something I'm lubing and tuning and expecting to perform at a high level, a clean level, a level I can be proud of. Maybe then people will see me and say, "Man, that guy can *ride*." Maybe then the hard winds will blow over the road, and I'll be able to help the group ride them out.

# 7

For twenty-two years, for as long as I've smoked cigarettes, I've been a huge fan of Samuel Beckett, the great Irish playwright and novelist. I say *fan* because I don't assess his writing in the way you might imagine an English professor would, that is to say with intellectual sophistication and scholarship and reasoned intelligence and its consequent penetrating worldview and so on and so on till you're bored blue. No way, dude.

I simply read the man's writing and I'm like totally wow, blown away, this stuff rocks!

Like this, just dig how vividly beauteous this is: _____

" . . . upper lake, with the punt, bathed off the bank, then pushed out into the stream and drifted. She lay stretched out on the floorboards with her hands under her head and her eyes closed. Sun blazing down, bit of a breeze, water nice and lively. I noticed a scratch on her thigh and asked her how she came by it. Picking gooseberries, she said. I said again I thought it was hopeless and no good going on, and she agreed, without opening her eyes."

That's from *Krapp's Last Tape*, which is, check this out, if you're looking for coincidences and signs and secret codes, a play that features a man on his *sixty*-ninth birthday listening to a reel-to-reel tape he made on his *thirty*-ninth birthday, on which he's talking about his *twenty*-ninth birthday. Pretty heavy, don't you think?

This is something the main character says on the tape, near the end of the play: "Perhaps my best years are gone. When there was a chance of happiness. But I wouldn't want them back. Not with the fire in me now. No, I wouldn't want them back."

And this, boys and girls, is my last cigarette. A Marlboro Medium, lit with a measure of joy and regret on this May 6, 2002, at a few minutes before midnight. I've been smoking a cigarette every ten minutes or so for the last few hours, roasting my way through my last pack, so many cigarettes today, and for the last few days, that my mouth resembles a dead volcano. The taste of my last cigarette, I can't describe it any other way, it's tasteless.

At midnight I'll turn thirty-nine and thereby pass into the fabled dramatic new phase of my time on earth, the middle-aged phase, the phase without the smoke cloud around me, the life instead where I'm the smoke-free man on a bicycle with a mission and a new set of lungs with which to accomplish it.

Quick thought: Is there a *bad* reason to quit smoking? 138,600.

That's the minimum number of cigarettes I've smoked in the last twenty-two years. Marlboro Mediums, my brand of choice for I think ten years, since they first came on the market. Smoked Camel Filters for the dozen years before that. Bummed a menthol occasionally, never have liked them much. I have always thought rolling your own was for the birds.

This sounds corny and predictable and as unoriginal a thought as could occur at a moment like this, but without cigarettes—this is one of my biggest worries—I won't be cool anymore. I won't be hip. I won't have that secret-society bond that occurs between smokers, say, when we're standing outside a doorway on a rainy day, a cold day, a day on which even a chicken would have the good sense to stay inside, but there we are, huddling together in exile and gathering nobility from the life we live smoking. Smokers, we say, are always the most interesting people, the ones with the most interesting stories to tell, maybe because there's something of a checkered past in the heart of every smoker.

How ridiculous. I'm worried I'll give up smoking and people are going to think I'm a dork.

But of all the bad habits I have, cigarettes represent the most profoundly dangerous to my future and at the same time the hardest of my horrible habits to eliminate. I quit cigarettes, my thinking goes, and the rest of my bad habits will fall like the house of cards they are.

Ah, these melodramatic drags, holding the smoke in like dope hits, exhaling it heavenward with great whooshes of exasperation, telling myself I'm giving this up for a noble reason, because I want to be a faster cyclist, I want to kick ass on the road, I don't want to get dropped anymore. That's it. I am tired of desperately trying to keep up.

True, if I give cigarettes up, it stands to reason a solid number of my current friends, well, they won't remain my friends in the way they've been, I won't be joining them being entertainingly deviant and interesting and all those things smokers are and that I've tried to be the whole time I've been a smoker.

My friends, my fellow smokers, they're out there in Carbondale tonight. I can hear them through my window, hundreds of ignitions going on at once, in the bars and on the front porches or the back stoops or here, at my desk, in my study, a few minutes before I turn thirty-nine, the itch of my lighter and the fire burning in my last cigarette for posterity.

My desk is a solid-core maple door propped on four-by-fours. I spend about half of my life sitting here. The door, the computer on it, the old stereo system on it, the couple of reference books, the ashtray, everything's covered, like Washington State after Mount St. Helen's erupted, with a thin layer of ash. In the window above the desk, I've got a built-in fan to blow the smoke out, been running constantly since my family moved in here, two years ago. Behind me, my smoke-eater grinds its eternal symphony to poor health and unhappiness.

A Marlboro Medium.

I smoke this one down all the way till the filter burns my fingertips. I don't need to mush it to death in the ashtray; it goes out on its own, a last small wisp and, like a life, it's over with.

Beckett writes, "Thirty-nine today, sound as a bell, apart from my old weakness, and intellectually I have now every reason to suspect at the . . . crest of the wave—or thereabouts."

For the next week I can't tell you my name if you ask me.

The semester ends, and I turn in my grades and conclude the business of the term—official records at Southern Illinois University will indicate that I've done this—but, much like a few years later, when the truck hits me and I spiral wildly through the air, I will never have a memory of arriving at the English Department and sitting in my office and filling out the grade sheets and strolling across the quadrangle with the other professors to the building where, as they say, we place that spring semester into the annals of history.

What I'll remember is riding and riding and riding and, when I'm not riding, cleaning my bike, I mean completely obsessively cleaning my bike, waxing the bike and buffing it and unwrapping the handlebar tape and polishing the bars, taking off cassettes and chainrings and chains and derailleurs and cables and disassembling anything else I can find on the bike and soaking it in solvent and removing every conceivable microscopic speck of grit and putting the bike back together and taking it out for a ride and oh no, it's dirty again, I've totally got to clean everything again!

I'll remember the exquisite afternoon sun, more brilliant than I've ever seen it, and the May flowers and the birds flying in circles over the roadside treetops, everything in Southern Illinois so green and so vivid, every day more vivid than the next, the heat from above seeping into the ground and radiating back from it.

And the nights, man, the nights.

I'm using the nicotine patch.

Wait a second. I have to stop right here and say *Don't quit without the patch*. It works. It's great. It's incredible in every way. I swear to God. And it's got a recreational-drug quality, too, for all those of you who are into that. Especially when you first start using the patch, wearing that big psychedelic 21-milligram dose, that's like wow, a *lot* of nicotine. On the box they come in, there's a warning about how this product can cause sleep disturbances and give you extremely vivid nightmares. I'm telling you right now, the package does not lie.

I dream ultra-crisp dreams. I dream so realistically that I wake up and believe what I'm dreaming has come true— for instance, that I'm still in middle school, in seventh grade and wearing a jean jacket, and I've got a test coming up in science class and I'm completely unprepared for the test, haven't studied for it at all, and I know my parents are going to be pissed and take away my bike for a week for flunking the test, and then I'm waking up in tears, genuinely bawling, and it takes me ten minutes to convince myself, man, you're thirty-nine years old, Mike, it doesn't matter if you can pass your seventh-grade science test when you're thirty-nine years old. Nobody's going to take away your bike.

Some days I'll try owning up to what's really going on. "Thirty-nine," I'll say. "I'm doing this because I can't handle turning thirty-nine." Then I'll try figuring out if not handling turning thirty-nine is a bad thing and conclude that it's not.

You're *supposed* to freak out when you turn thirty-nine. It's like standing next to a cliff; you're *supposed* to be scared.

If I'm about to break down and buy a pack or maybe bum a smoke off of somebody, I'll literally sit down and write out every step of my plan to become a better cyclist, and remind myself that, even if it's the wrong plan, it's the only one I have, and I've got to go through all of these steps if I'm going to achieve my goal.

In exact order:

1. Quit smoking.
2. Go someplace where there's a really big mountain and see if I can ride up it. Because a cyclist needs something there, of course. A cyclist needs a mountain. My pick: Beech Mountain in North Carolina, a mountain made famous in Lance Armstrong's book *It's Not About the Bike.* It's a ten-hour drive from my house to the base of Beech Mountain—not all that far away, really—and I doubt I can ride to the summit on my first attempt, but sooner or later I'll do it. Why not?
3. Sign up for a one-hundred-mile charity ride, a century ride. Because I've been reading *Bicycling* magazine for at least fifteen years, and every spring they run a big feature on how to train for and complete one of these century rides. I guess that's always sounded cool to me but for one reason or another, one excuse or another, I haven't done one.
4. Quit drinking. This is with the proviso that the quitting-smoking thing is a success.
5. Quit eating.
6. Survive all this, take the bike out, and kick people's asses.

# HEFT ON WHEELS

Okay, I know I'm crazy, and I know I *want* to be crazy because being crazy is a vast improvement over being a smoker, not to say there aren't crazy smokers, but you know what I mean. There is absolutely nothing wrong with being crazy if being crazy is calculated to foster a greater good. Better yet, maybe a person has to go crazy for a while in order to become sane.

Along these lines, let me mention that I've been a fan of Phil Liggett for many years, though not so many years as I've been smoking. Phil Liggett being, if you're not a cyclist or a cycling fan you won't know, the famed voice of the Tour de France, which I've been following religiously since the days of Greg LeMond, watching it in half-hour segments on ESPN in the middle of the night. For as long as I can remember riding bikes, I've been pretending Phil Liggett is providing play-by-play for my efforts on the road. I can always hear Phil saying, "Oh, the powerful sprinter Mike Magnuson takes the field at the line." Or "Magnuson is really putting his rivals in difficulty today." Or, on one of my numerous bad days, "The best Magnuson can do now is ride to limit his losses."

I pretend I'm in a TV commercial for Trek bicycles, standing there big and strong and well-adjusted and doing an oh-shucks thing with my shoulders and saying, "Anyway, I bought the Trek 5200 because over the years, owing to my size"—explaining how, because of my weight, I've visited such horrors upon my poor bicycles that it's a

miracle some of them haven't tried escaping me and joining the circus, how I've broken spokes on every wheel type
imaginable, broken frames and forks and handlebars and
seat posts and saddles and cranks and bottom brackets and
pedals and worn through tires at three times the rate of a
normal, non-250-pound cyclist. Saying, "So I was looking
for an exceptionally fat-guy-proof bike"—grasping my
bike by the top tube and raising it up for the camera to
see, shiny black carbon fiber, beautiful and beautifully
bombproof— "and I got one!"

I pretend I hear applause. I pretend Trek's sending me
free bikes.

Some of my nightmares are true nightmares, real things,
really horrible memories, like one Saturday morning near
the end of last season, I rode on a Saturday morning with a
fellow named Ed Erickson, a tall skinny guy who is legendary in these parts for being a great climber. He's
extremely lean, maybe 150 pounds, with a bony face and
bony arms and legs and a way of jerking uphill on a bike
that makes him closely resemble the famous gaunt Spanish
climber Fernando Escartin, a rider who's given none other
than Lance Armstrong trouble on plenty of mountainous
occasions.

"Not a pretty sight," Phil Liggett would say, "but he's
certainly giving it a credible go on the Col today."

Ed and I took a forty-two-mile loop called Rocky
Comfort, the middle part of which features a ten-mile

stretch of incredibly steep rollers and dangerous wooden bridges and sharp potholed curves. Rocky Comfort's as tough a route as we have around here—steep climb after steep climb on bad chip-and-seal pavement; no way to build momentum on descents because of the danger of crashing, so you're always starting each hill from a near dead stop, from scratch. The only safe place to attack on Rocky Comfort, therefore, is on the climbs, which is what Ed did. He attacked the stuffing out of me. Every uphill, he kicked my butt. He stomped me so badly he would climb to the top of a hill, roll back down it, and climb to the top again before I could crest it for the first time.

I got pissed at Ed, too. I told him, "You don't have to rub it in my face, man."

He told me I shouldn't be pissed, that he's just trying to get some exercise.

A few days later, on group ride, when we were heading up the first hill out of Carbondale, the very hill on Dogwood where in two years I will ride over it first and then smash into a Dodge Dakota, Ed rode up behind me, put a hand on my back, and started pushing me uphill.

That broke me. All that riding I'd done, all that money I'd put into it, I hadn't gotten anywhere. I quit riding with the group for the season right then and there.

Or how about this for a true-to-life nightmare:

Once upon a time Moby consumed about twice the quantity of plankton his body required to swim happily in the sea. If he were going for a forty-mile bike ride, for example, he'd typically sit down three hours beforehand and inhale a giant bowl of cold pasta with olive oil and a can of tuna and croutons and grated cheese and a couple of handfuls of cashews and an avocado and some tomato slices and maybe a hard-boiled egg, if one was handy. Wash that down with a twenty-four-ounce glass of Endurox R4, with a couple of bananas for dessert and maybe, closer to the ride itself, ten oatmeal cookies and some grapes or a nectarine or whatever else managed to survive in the vast wasteland of Moby's fruit basket. This isn't to mention, during the ride, drinking two twenty-four-ounce bottles of Accelerade and eating a PowerBar and one or two PowerGels. After the ride: more Endurox R4. And maybe a big bowl of ice cream before bed, because a cyclist can eat anything, right? And a cyclist can drink beer at the bar a few nights a week? And on the way home from the bar stop at La Bamba's for a Burrito As Big As Your Head?

Quitting. I don't need to experience nicotine withdrawal to know how intensely pathetic the idea of quitting is, but my tragic flaw, I can see this during my delirium, has always been that I'm a quitter. I allow myself to get discouraged too easily. I take getting beaten as a sign I will never be able to win.

I am often mean to my students. I say their work is slipshod or pointless or stupid or, what's usually the case,

they're not working hard enough at it. When I am mean, I
try to say, "Sorry, I'm just doing my job. I'm trying to help
you improve." I say that the only rule I know for improving
is this: *We learn by getting our asses kicked.*

Then I say, if you want to do this the simplest, least
humiliating way, you must first learn how to kick your
own ass.

# 8

$A$ couple of weeks after the nicotine hallucinations have faded and thirty-nine has wrapped around me like an itchy sweater, I take my wife and kids with me on the typical American midlife-crisis-slash-cycling-pilgrimage weekend trip from our home in southern Illinois to the town that Lance Armstrong made famous: Boone, North Carolina.

To get there, a ten-hour drive, with screaming kids.

Wait, have I mentioned that my wife has quit smoking on the same day I quit? That we're quitting together? And she's wearing the same patches I am and she's totally flipping out, too?

97

I mean, how could I forget to mention *that*?

I'm too wacko is why, and so is my wife. Not her fault, not mine. We're doing the right thing, quitting together, and absolutely if you want to quit smoking, see if another of your fellow smokers will quit at the same time as you, but for goodness' sake, don't make the mistake my wife and I make on the ten-hour trip to Boone.

We've left Carbondale before dawn and haven't changed our patches since the previous day, meaning, by the time we've been on the road for a few hours and the children are bored and carsick and fighting with each other, my wife and I are plumb out of nicotine. We're strung out, salivating, irritable, nauseated on the steep winding mountain roads over from east Tennessee into the North Carolina high country, and what am I trying to say here? This trip really sucks so far, but hey, isn't it *neat* the family will come along with me while I do this?

See, I'm drawn to Boone, like many cyclists before me, because I know by heart the legend of Lance here, the story millions have read in his book *It's Not About the Bike*, the part where Lance has survived cancer and returned to European road racing, only to lose heart and quit and return home and play golf and go to the bar every day. He says he's not going to make it back into competition. He says he's fat and out of shape and hanging out in a Mexican restaurant drinking beer and feeling hopeless. But his coach, Chris Carmichael, gives him a call and persuades

Lance to give cycling a go one last time. Lance comes here to Boone then, heads out to train on a miserable, frigid, steady-raining spring day and rides six horrible hours in a bone-chilling springtime mountain fog; can't see anything, can't feel anything but hurt; then he's climbing Beech Mountain, lifting up his pace, hammering, finding a new meaning in his life. Who among us hasn't been inspired by Lance on that day? When he realizes he's "meant for a long, hard climb," isn't that awesome?

Playing the role of Lance's coach, Chris Carmichael, will be my wife and two daughters, who will be waiting for me at strategic points along the climb, either to shout encouragement or to pull me out of the ditch when I collapse into it, which is to say, people, that this will be actual climbing I'm doing. This will not be a trick I'm performing for the cameras.

Next morning I'm mounted on my trusty Trek 5200 and rolling through the town of Banner Elk, past Lees McCrae College, turning onto NC 184, the very road where Lance's mystical climbing experience took place, the road up to the summit of Beech Mountain, five thousand feet in the air.

The sky's not particularly Lancelike this morning; it's as dry as an old skeleton. Hasn't rained in weeks. They're having a bad drought in North Carolina and have been for a couple of summers now. Everyone hereabouts, I've been told, is praying for rain, but as far as I'm concerned, the rain can hold off a little while longer. There's nothing I hate more than riding my bike in the rain.

But after a few hundred yards of upward road, I wouldn't know if the sky has fallen or has turned tropical-storm green or if I've been transported to Pluto and left there to suffer forever. Climbing Beech Mountain is carnage and degradation and unspeakable agony; this is supreme misery just to take one pedal stroke; this is the all-time worst suffering I've ever undergone on a bicycle. The road is an endless wall in front of me, climbing and climbing to somewhere I can't see.

A third of the way up, at a coughing, nearly-puking five miles per hour, I pass my family. My six-year-old daughter says, "Are you okay, daddy?"

"I'm fine," I say. "I'm reliving my youth."

I'm seeing colors and drooling and thinking how happy I was eating donuts and drinking coffee in my hotel room this morning and oh, how easy things were, truly, before I read Lance Armstrong's *It's Not About the Bike* and got all carried away with this turn-myself-into-a-real-cyclist thing.

Quitting, there's quitting again. I think about never riding a bicycle again, never even *thinking* about a bicycle again.

I leave my body for a long while and see heaven, a place with a nicely paved flat road and a tailwind and a light fog surrounding me. I'm emerging into a cloud bank at Beech Mountain's crest and rolling to a stop in the same gravel parking lot where I'm certain, on that legendary day of yore, Lance met Chris Carmichael and said, "Give me my rain jacket, I'm riding back."

Lance may have become a better man on this climb, but me: I'm choked up, crying, bubbled over with accomplishment and at the same time grief and irreparable loss. I hadn't believed I could make it up this mountain on my first try, and now that I have, I realize I'm trying to kill the person I have been in order to become somebody else, and I can see now that I'm going to succeed.

Nevertheless, I say to my wife, "Take my bike, I'm *driving* back."

A few days later, six hundred miles west of Boone, in the comfort of my La-Z-Boy, I take the philosophical view of my experience on Beech Mountain. Like this: Wow! I actually climbed Beech Mountain! I made it all the way to the top and didn't get off my bike, not *once!* They can take everything I own, buddy, but they can't take it from me that I climbed Beech Mountain on my bicycle. That's a hell of an accomplishment for a doddering thirty-nine-year-old fart like me.

From this kind of deep philosophizing I arrive at the following logical conclusion: I should go out with my bike and do something even *harder*. Preferably *much* harder.

Of course, it doesn't take long to find something like that. I punch up Google and enter a string of search terms:

*True Suffering + Gruelingly Steep Hills + Impossible for Mere Mortals + Worst Climbing Imaginable + North Carolina.*

What pops up is this picture, taken on a sunny day, of two cyclists struggling up the steepest paved road I've ever seen. The rider in the foreground looks like if he stops pedaling he'll pitch over backward. The rider behind him is weaving in a zigzag up the grade to keep from falling off his bike—it's just so amazingly steep. The road behind the two riders drops off like a cliff. You can see a car on the switchback corner down below, and the car looks very, very small.

Here's the picture's caption: *Bridge to Bridge Incredible Cycling Challenge. 100 Miles of Pure Hill.*

Ask, as the old saying goes, and ye shall receive.

Turns out the distance of the Bridge to Bridge Incredible Cycling Challenge is slightly longer than one hundred miles, and even though each rider is timed and is given a place among the six hundred or so other riders who manage to finish, the Bridge to Bridge is not a race per se. It's what's called a challenge century, meaning a seriously strenuous event with major climbing in it, an epic ride even for the fittest of riders, definitely *not* one of those fun-for-charity thingies where you can show up with the family—kids on trikes and Big Wheels and so on—for a relaxing flat Sunday spin with pizza and hot dogs and Cokes and face-painting stations along the route.

This is what you do for the Bridge to Bridge: You line up with nine hundred cyclists for a mass start at the mall in

# HEFT ON WHEELS

Lenoir, North Carolina, elevation 1,081 feet, at the base of
the Blue Ridge Mountains, and you go up and down and
around for the next hundred miles. If you're fit and my
guess is if you're lucky, you'll finish at the summit of Grandfather Mountain, elevation 5,280 feet, a mile high, the
highest point in the Blue Ridge. The total elevation gain
for the course is 6,800 feet by some accounts, 10,000 by
others—lots of *up* however you look at it—and those last
2.5 miles, the 1,180-foot ascent of Grandfather's switchbacks, represent one of the pinnacles of suffering in American recreational cycling. It's the hardest, the most awful,
the most humbling finish there is. Do this, survive it, and
you'll be the real deal.

Well, yeah, whatever. I've got some other things to
survive in the meantime.

**9**

I keep riding a couple of hours a day, six days a week.

Do some studying, too. I bone up on the relationship between diet and exercise and between pain and suffering. In particular, I read and reread a short story called "The Hunger Artist," by Franz Kafka.

"No one could possibly watch the hunger artist continuously, day and night," Kafka writes, "and so no one could produce first-hand evidence that the fast had really been rigorous and continuous; only the artist himself could know that, he was therefore bound to be the sole completely satisfied spectator of his own fast."

Because that's exactly what I'll have to do. I've been making it so far with the no-smoking, and I've made it up Beech Mountain; this means, sooner or later, I'll have to go on the epic diet to end all epic diets. I'm thinking, when the time comes, I'll maintain my same riding schedule but only consume three 550-calorie protein shakes a day, putting me into your basically horrendous calorie-to-output deficit. How I've come up with the protein-shake idea, I don't know. Too much late-night TV probably. But the calorie-to-output deficit, I've learned that from Franz Kafka.

"Just try to explain the art of fasting!" Kafka writes. "Anyone who has no feeling for it cannot be made to understand it."

I am a realistic person. I'm not expecting too much. I go ahead and sign up for one of those fun-for-charity centuries, one of those that's a very distant, distant lowland relative of the Bridge to Bridge. I do the Trek 100 in Pewaukee, Wisconsin, near my hometown, in the first week of June, and I get all nervous about whether I can finish it or not, but it's no problem at all. I finish in well under six hours, and in all the training charts and goal charts on century training in *Bicycling* magazine, they'll tell you if you can ride a century in under six hours, you have ridden very well. You can be proud of yourself.

After the ride, I tell myself I'm going to take one more month to keep doing what I've been doing, riding every day and focusing on getting over quitting cigarettes, then

I'm going to quit drinking and quit eating on the same day.
I pick July 8 for the date of my execution, the Monday after
Independence Day, and this is because I've always loved
getting bombed on Independence Day. I want to have one
last good time.

So I have my good time, July 8 comes, and I discover that
I weigh 235 pounds. In two months, just from riding a lot,
I've lost twenty pounds, and let me tell you, that's exactly
the motivation I need to go for broke.

In the next seven days I lose five pounds, then five
pounds the next week, and the next week after that.

I come to understand what the Wicked Witch is
thinking at the end. "What a world!" she says.

What a world indeed. I'm living these melting weeks
in a constant delirium and with a nagging desire to steal
candy from babies or pies from window sills or hamburgers
from backyard grills. If I ride my bike past La Bamba's, I
burst into tears. If I see a dog chomping on a pot-roast
bone or even a robin extracting a worm from the ground, I
get depressed and jealous. I ride alone in the countryside
and hold profound discourses on the vicissitudes of gas-
tronomy: the joys of lasagna! the excellence of nachos! the
Nobel Prize–worthy aspects of Pizza Hut's lunchtime
buffet!

One afternoon I'm carrying on in such a manner, muttering something insightful like "I really, really think peach
pie is magnificent," and I look up from the road to see an

old man standing in a ditch. He smiles at me and says, "Who doesn't?" I'll never be certain if the old man was actually there or if I was just hallucinating him.

Once, when my six-year-old daughter wants a sip of my midday protein shake, I say, "Never! It's *mine!*" I have to wait eight hours till my next shake, and I don't care who she is or how cute she is; she's not getting one drop of my lunch.

Somewhere in there, I crack. I get weak and can't go on. I drag my wife with me to Red Lobster on a Thursday evening, when the place is packed, and we have to wait for a half hour in the foyer, holding a little beeper. While we wait, I become irrational and keep telling my wife that I want to take the young skinny fellow in charge of seating and stick his head in the lobster tank just to demonstrate to him precisely what it was like, at that instant, to be me. When we finally get into the dining room, I order the biggest item on the menu, what they call the Admiral's Feast, a colossal plate of various fried things, and, owing to the emptiness of my gut and the long time it has been since I've eaten solid food, let along *fried* solid food, before my wife and I could leave Red Lobster, I have to make an emergency restroom stop the violence of which would startle Montezuma himself.

Oh, Phil Liggett! Where are you when I need you most? Why don't you enter the broadcast of my agony and say, "That's a nasty bit of dieting Magnuson's doing"? Or

"The Big Swede's really suffering like a dog out there. Every part of his body must be screaming in pain!"?

I can feel my guts consuming themselves whenever I ride, an inner slurping feeling, like a sci-fi flick's gelatinous blob squishing through a spaceship's ventilator system, and I can taste something alkaline on my tongue, the taste of old food, the cheeseburgers and milkshakes and megaton pasta salads of days long gone. Not to mention the Beer Gut Itself, the years and years of beer stored up inside me, the afternoon beer and the beer after supper and the beer before bed. Think of the calories that amounts to. Fifteen hundred calories a day? Two thousand? In beer alone? For how many years? I'm surprised I don't get drunk in the process of consuming myself.

But I don't get drunk. I don't want to get drunk. It's not like I'm having the DTs or anything. I'm totally freaking about starving too much to have the DTs probably. I am only able to add up my collection of addiction-withdrawal experiences into one uniform fear: I'm thinking one beer means I'll have ten beers, and having ten beers means I'll get weak and bum a smoke off of somebody, and if I bum a smoke, I'll buy a pack and then a carton, and no, no, no. I don't eat. I don't drink. I don't smoke. That's it. That's about all I can wrap my mind around.

Because it's working. Cyclists are forever talking about upgrading their bike parts to lighten their bikes a few hundred *grams* to improve their climbing. Try taking fifty or sixty or seventy *pounds* off the *cyclist* and see what happens. You will climb hills—as Richard Virenque said of Lance Armstong's crushing attack on the rainy road up to Hautacam in the 2000 Tour de France—"like a jet plane taking off."

That's been the secret for Lance, right? The guy loses fifteen pounds and retains the same power, and he becomes an invincible climbing machine. Sixty pounds off of me? Unreal. I mean completely unreal. I can all of a sudden hang with anybody in town. I really can fly. E.T.'s got nothing on me. Nobody can drop me, and if they do, it's because I don't catch a draft when it's there for the taking or don't accelerate at the proper time or just plain don't understand how cyclists work together on the road to go faster. But how could I know? I've never been up front on a group ride before.

Sixth week of this, of losing *five pounds* per week, when I'm at two hundred pounds or so, I chow down a couple of PowerBars and a banana, put Accelerade in my bottles, tuck a couple of PowerGels in the back of my jersey, and roll off to the Wednesday night group ride with the proverbial full tank of fuel and looking to go out and grind people under my tires, and prove, after all these fat years, I'm now the King of the Road.

Kafka writes, "It could happen, especially when he

had been fasting for some time, that he reacted with an outburst of fury and to the general alarm began to shake the bars of his cage like a wild animal."

At the Carbondale Cycle parking lot, where the group rides begin, Ed Erickson's present and accounted for, all bones and muscle, the spitting image of Fernando Escartin. Ed's a nice fellow. He paints houses for a living and does quality work and would never think of ripping anybody off. He goes to church on Sunday morning before he rides. If anybody gets a flat, Ed's always the first person to stop and offer assistance. He's the type of person you want your kids to be like when they grow up. But there in the parking lot I see Ed, a person who is naturally skinny, and I'm thinking I've been starving myself for weeks and riding too much and getting grumpy too often and that all of this suffering is supposed to culminate in me destroying Ed, maybe making him cry or something. I don't look him in the eye, don't nod hello.

In half an hour, after we've warmed up on the way out of town, we hit the first long climb of the day, Honker Hill, named, they say, after the geese that travel through southern Illinois every fall and spring, and I attack Ed with everything I've got.

I can't drop him, not yet. But I'm hurting him. He sits behind me, sucking air, for eight miles. When we get to the checkpoint where the leaders always let the rest of the group catch up, we stop, we're the leaders, and I wait to hear Phil Liggett froth over my victory. Instead, I hear Ed say, "Man, that was fun."

And, oh, it is.

That evening I fill out my entry forms for the Bridge to Bridge and send them in.

# 10

I don't know. I say that a lot, now that I'm thirty-nine years old. I don't know. When I was *twenty*-nine, I used to say *I know*. I used to have things all figured out. Part of turning *thirty*-nine, I guess, is finally recognizing that nothing in the world happens like you planned it, which means if you embark on a ridiculous summerlong quest like giving up drinking and smoking and losing a lot of weight and preparing for the Bridge to Bridge Incredible Cycling Challenge, you'll understand from the get-go that you don't really know what you're getting into till you get into it. That's of course exactly why people embark on quests in the first place, because they don't know.

I don't know.

I don't know what the course for the Bridge to Bridge looks like, what the road surface is like on it, how horrible the climbs might be beyond what they look like on paper or beyond the way they've been described in accounts I can find on the Internet.

I find quite a few accounts, people detailing their experience in every phase: how they felt the day before, what they ate the day before, what their buddies ate the day before, the weather the morning of the event, where the best places are to pee along the route. People describe trying to conserve their energy for the first fifty miles, which is a loop from Lenoir toward Hickory and back and then out Old Adako Road to NC 181, elevation 1,097 feet, because once you're on NC 181 you're in the "pure hill" portion of the ride. In the next twenty miles, the course rises to the Blue Ridge Parkway, to the Grandmother Mountain Overlook, 4,400 feet, and then plunges down the Linville Viaduct, through the breathtaking Linville Gorge and into Blowing Rock, then rising back up NC 221 to the Grandfather Mountain park entrance, where all accounts concur that this is where the real agony begins, on that 2.5-mile, 1,180-feet ascent straight up to a mile high in the air.

To be honest with you, I wouldn't know.

I don't have mountains where I live. Got plenty of hills, though. An endless supply of Ozark-style steep-grade rollers on winding, potholed chip-and-seal that's not much better than dirt. We have dozens and dozens of climbs here of one hundred feet, two hundred feet, even seven hundred feet, and I figure if you ride for a hundred miles through this terrain you'll have climbed at least three thousand feet. Maybe it's four thousand. It's a lot, in any event, and will prepare me for the challenge to come. It hurts to ride where I live, which means it goes without saying I've got buddies who, like me, are experiencing the pesky symptoms of either early-onset or full-blown middle age and are one-hundred-percent thrilled to go suffering with me in these hills whenever opportunity presents itself—like six days a week, covering a distance of at least 250 miles.

Gerald the carpenter. Fred the oral surgeon. Saki the bike-shop owner. Mike the English professor. Don the psychologist. Ed the house painter. Darren the sociologist.

My buddy Don the psychologist, a guy I ride with a few times a week, he's an avid birdwatcher when he's not on the bike, and he says this summer, for the first time in his life, he's spotted the rare Red-necked Phalarope, which is not the large fellow in the John Deere cap driving that pickup we seem to see everywhere in southern Illinois. The Red-necked Phalarope is a small shore bird that displays the peculiar behavioral characteristic of endlessly spinning in circles in search of food. By all accounts, the Red-necked Phalarope is approximately thirty-nine years old.

For all any of us know, we've been seeing lots of birds that might be Red-necked Phalaropes along the road in the high summer heat. I don't have time for that, though, because, boy, I've got what a cyclist needs to have a successful season: an epic event to train for.

So I'm doing lots of suffering with the other old farts and staying up late at night studying maps and reading accounts of the Bridge to Bridge, and in the day, when I'm supposed to be working, I do stuff like gather the nerve to call Cathy Rhuberg, the person who coordinates the Bridge to Bridge. I ask her if she thinks I'll make it. I can hear the smile in her voice when tells me, "Most of them do."

She gets me in touch with a guy named Greg Wilson, who's finished the Bridge to Bridge each of the thirteen times it's been held and who's famous, according to Cathy, for riding with a rubber pig on his helmet. He's known, she tells me, as the Animal. Some summers, Greg's ridden ten thousand miles. He's ridden tough centuries all over the world. He's a tough, intimidating rider. But when I talk to him, he's not too scary. Amused is what he is. I tell him I've never done something like this, and I'm training hard, and wow, I'm scared about making it, and he tells me scared is good. He tells me it's going to hurt, really hurt. I don't believe he thinks I'm going to make it, particularly when he says the Bridge to Bridge is much harder than it looks like on paper. His best time is seven and a half hours, which sounds impressive to me. After I talk to him, I decide if I can finish in, like, nine hours, and come in 550th place, I'll have acquitted myself admirably.

I don't know.

One day my buddy Darren puts a videotape into my hands and says, "This'll inspire you." It's the classic cycling film *A Sunday in Hell*, directed by Jorgen Leth, a documentary of the 1976 Paris–Roubaix race, featuring Eddy Merckx and Francesco Moser and some other legends of European cycling. The text on the back of the video reads, "Over 90 minutes of finely calculated suspense that leaves the viewer limp from vicarious excitement and pain."

Whew! Sounds steamy. And it is. We've got abundant slow-motion race footage, accompanied by an all-male operatic choir slowly singing, with much dignity and melancholy, "Paris–Roubaix." We've got dust, sun, cobbles, crashes, road rash and broken bones, futile attacks, suffering, sadness, joy. An awesome flick, in my estimation. But when I get done watching it, I give Darren a call and say, "Where are the hills? And isn't it supposed to be raining for Paris–Roubaix?"

Paris–Roubaix, you see, it's best known for being wet and muddy. That's the kind of thing I've known for years, the terminology of European bicycle racing, that whole world in my imagination that I have played out while I'm riding. Always a dream, I think, but now I've actually become a fast cyclist, and that style of go-for-broke hard riding, I'm actually riding that way now. My buddy Darren, this guy's a real racer, fastest and fittest cyclist in Carbondale, and I'm riding with him several days a week now, and keeping up. Couple of years ago, you would have told me

I'd be keeping up with the fastest rider in town, I never would have believed you.

Pretty cool, don't you think?

The Sunday of Labor Day weekend, a couple of weeks before the Bridge to Bridge, I take off for a long one with my old nemesis-slash-buddy Ed, a hard ride, too, east of town, into the steepest most numerous hills of the Shawnee, rise after rise, charging dog after charging dog emerging from the ramshackle dirt yards and beat-down trailers along the tore-up road. We contest every hill, dueling it out side by side, wheeling-up each other all day, Ed by a wheel-length on one hill, me by a wheel-length the next, flat-out beating the crap out of each other. But is this not the essence of hardcore cycling? We're out here pummeling each other and not giving each other an inch.

All this summer, that's been where I've been heading, transformation, becoming the man who Ed cannot drop, and now I'm with him tooth and nail, tire to tire, ashes to ashes, dust to dust, and I've arrived. I'm a new man. I've ground the man I've been into a vapor I can hardly remember. I've been riding thousands of miles this summer, averaging 250 miles a week, starving the hell out of myself, devoting every waking moment to bicycling, if not riding, thinking about riding, and what they call this in sports, folks, is focus. And focus is a beautiful thing. And hanging with Ed, that's what we call *results*.

A couple days later, Wednesday group ride, five-thirty in the Carbondale Cycle parking lot. A nice typical early September night in southern Illinois. Bit of a breeze, temperature in the mid-seventies, et cetera. Ed's here and Darren and Gerald and Don and a bunch of the college kids. The kids are back for the fall semester, and I guess it's true that I've been preparing all summer to meet these kids on the asphalt and duel with them and make them pant like dogs and in turn, because I'm twenty years older, I can feel better than them, because that's what I've been up to all summer, right? Feeling better? Feeling stronger than others? Superior?

Ben is one of the kids, and on the way out Dogwood toward the sign that says "Why will ye die?", he's already going fast, and it's pissing me off that he's already going fast. My legs are killing me and my gut hurts because I've actually eaten something this afternoon and the acids inside me must have atrophied or something. I don't think I've taken a day off the bike in at least three weeks. I'm trashed.

But Ben. The kid feels nothing. He's six feet two and bird-boned and wearing full bike kit, including cleated shoes, he weighs 145 pounds. Doesn't look like a strong kid but he's got the best pedal stroke in town, perfect circles, legs straight up and down. The kid's the real deal.

"Dammit," I say, way too loud, so everybody around me can hear. "That punk kid shouldn't be hammering during the warmup period." Nobody says anything. "Piss me off," I say. Everybody keeps pedaling. "I need time to get my old bones uncreaked here."

This isn't a rule, this is fact: *Nobody wants to hear you whine.*

We get to the Spillway and gradually pick up steam on the long sloping downhill toward Honker Hill and our destinies. Picking it up good. We're together in a long line, Darren and Ben ahead, Gerald, Don, Ed, and this new kid Eric on an old Trek 2300 aluminum bike, everyone's tires and gears hiss, the sound of fifteen cyclists cruising tempo at thirty miles per hour, and in the archway of trees along the Spillway the cicadas drone, and I believe I can hear their voices transmogrifying from insect to English to the French I imagine professional bike racers speak to each other.

Go, go, go, they say.

*Allez, allez, allez.*

*Vite, vite.*

*Allons-y.*

The classic attack point, as on so many group rides heretofore, is on the lower slopes of Honker Hill, and what Darren does, he maintains the same speed the group's been traveling in the flat when we start rising. Results: Darren and Ben break off the front, and the rest of the group strings out into a shambles.

However. And this is the great thing, that I can say *however*, because to say that means I am not going to ease off, I will not be beaten here, I'm going to dig deep inside my guts and surge through all the hurt and misfortune and I'm going to catch Darren and Ben. And I do it. I close the gap they've created, and in the process, I pull the rest of the group forward to them, which is great: I've become an asset to the group after all.

Then the second step of the ladder toward Giant City Road begins, and Darren and Ben go off the front again, and I suck it up and deal with the fact I've been dropped and dig back inside myself and hammer forward again, so deep my ears ring and I can't tell if the ringing is constant cicadas in the trees or some form of high-pressure gas escaping through my ears, and I pull the group back to Darren and Ben again.

I say to Ben, "You ain't much, you young puppy, if you can't drop us old guys."

He says something about my weight, and I'm pretty sure it's not that he's noticed I lost any. I believe he tells me I'm old and fat.

In any case, before I can take offense, Darren attacks again and Ben follows, and the group, the poor group, they who suffer so much while these dramas play out before them, we get obliterated. Too much this time, we'll never catch them to the top, but hey, we can limit our losses, right, we can at least dial ourselves up to the same speed Darren and Ben are going, and that way we won't get dropped any worse than we've already been dropped.

Phil Liggett says, "The best Magnuson can do in this stage is ride to limit his losses."

Only Ed and this new kid Eric on the aluminum Trek 2300 make it with me, and I'm hurting bad, I'm blown, I'm experiencing this screaming-pain thing that cyclists are always speaking of with great fondness and zeal, and I don't believe I can drive this train much longer, got to draft and recover for a minute or two, so I pull off the line to let the kid do some work, and when he passes me, he doesn't register I'm letting him so I can draft off *him* and catch my breath.

He shakes his head and says, "I understand how you're feeling, man."

I breathe hard and say, "Like how?"

He says, "I've just taken a couple of weeks off the bike, too."

What can I say? I don't know.

# 11

At 6:00 a.m., September 15, an hour before dawn and the start of the 2002 Bridge to Bridge Incredible Cycling Challenge, I do know something: I know that rain is falling on my head, right here, in the Lenoir Mall parking lot. Bigtime rain. Hammering-down rain. And the forecast is for harder and harder and harder till maybe it'll be time to call for an ark. The cause for this is Tropical Storm Hanna, which twenty-four hours ago made landfall at Mobile Bay, Alabama, along the Gulf of Mexico, and has moved in an absolutely direct path to Lenoir, North Carolina, where it's fixing to drop in the range of _____

three to five inches between here and Grandfather Mountain today.

The temperature's not bad, though, near seventy, and the rain doesn't seem so bad, other than it's there and steady and the whole world's making a hissing sound. I coast on my bike through the parking lot, up and down the rows of cars and past the cyclists getting ready—predominantly men my age or thereabouts: some with their wives or girlfriends standing dutifully by with the water bottle or the pump or the helmet; some checking and rechecking equipment; some putting on and then taking off rain jackets. Nobody's joking. I can't hear laughter anywhere. Once in a while a fellow will yell out, "It's Paris–Roubaix today, boys." Which will be followed shortly by muted groans that fade into the sloshing-down of tropical drizzle around us.

I bump into Greg Wilson, the Animal, who indeed wears a rubber pig atop his helmet, and he's in a good mood. The pig looks to be in a good mood, too. No complaints. Rain ain't nothing to either man or pig. Greg's with his parents, nice people, confident in their son's ability to survive the ordeal coming on. They don't tell him this endeavor is desperate—you're going to get hurt out there, son. Nope. When I ask if they're worried about him, they tell me he can ride through anything and has done so for years and years, but they wish me luck.

Eventually daylight fades into the rain, and the ride

begins. The Animal's riding next to me out of the parking lot and along the first mile of flat straightaway, but when we take the first short two-hundred-foot climb out of Lenoir, Greg drops behind me. I figure he'll catch me and pass me later, but he never does.

Everything's water hissing under tires and bikes spraying cold fantails of grit, and no rider talks, not that I can hear over the rain and my concentrating on what I'm doing so I don't slip and crash. Once in a while, a rider will start to talk, to say there's a car up or a car back, if there is one, but nothing much except wet cyclists moves on the road today. No cars. No people lining the ride route. Not even the dogs have come out to chase us today. Somewhere out there the mountains loom, but nobody here can see them.

I think I've known all summer, maybe my whole life, that epic is as epic does, that however long the odds and impossible the goal may seem, this is no reason to sit on the couch and say it can't be done. I ride the first fifty miles in a tropical downpour, I've ridden all summer to avoid a thirty-nine-year-old downslide, and when I start the first major climb of the Bridge to Bridge, up NC 181, from its intersection with Old Adako Road at 1,097 feet to Old Jonas Ridge School at 3,750 feet, when the grade won't go away and the higher and higher I get the colder and colder and foggier and foggier the air gets, till I'm literally in the clouds and can't see a thing except the ghost forms of the riders strung along the road above me, this is when I understand what great good happens when human beings climb mountains on bicycles. We do not climb the mountain because it's there; we climb it because we can.

After a long while I see a man sprawled in the ditch next to his nice Colnago C-40, and there's so much rain falling that the ditch is a small river flowing around him. He's gripping a PowerBar but not getting it anywhere near his mouth.

I ask him, "Are you okay?"

He smiles at me and says, "Yeah, I'm fine."

High in the mountains now. Temperatures must have dropped fifteen degrees, maybe twenty, from what they were this morning, three thousand feet below, down in Lenoir, and I've been soaked to the skin and getting pelted heavily for four hours now, for five hours now, for six hours now. My thighs are periodically cramping, and I'm very cold. I'm connected through my cleats and pedals to my bicycle, which has become as much a part of me as my heart and lungs.

Up Grandfather, the rain's falling as hard as it has all day, a steady thick-drop battering, and nearly an inch of water flows downward over the asphalt. The steepness of the road is the stuff of legend, and the wind and rain and wholesale desperation are unimaginable: People are stopping, getting off their bikes and pushing them, or simply sitting in the ditch and placing their heads in their hands—but I don't stop pedaling. The Red-necked Phalarope spins endlessly in circles because that is what he's meant to do on

Earth; I ride my bicycle because that's what I'm meant to do. I'll never stop pedaling. I'm a middle-aged man now, and that's nothing to be ashamed of or afraid of. I keep rising, passing other cyclists who are no doubt experiencing similar ecstasies of hurt and self-understanding, and even though I'm climbing toward a thing I cannot see, passing through the clouds toward the firmament, I know I've got somewhere to get to. I know I'm happy.

When I reach the summit and cross the finish line and roll to a stop, an event volunteer takes my bicycle from me so it can be put into a truck and taken safely down the mountain, and when the bicycle slips from my hands and the worker wheels it away into the rainy mountaintop distance, I burst into tears.

Mike Magnuson
Rider # 276
6 hours 28 mins 36 seconds
146th rider to finish

# 12

Let us gather and drop our pretenses and clear a few mysteries:

Saki does not own Carbondale Cycle. His brother Somchai does, but you never really see Somchai around the shop, just once in a while he'll hunker in and sit at a table in the back room and read the stock-market page of the *Southern Illinoisan* and make no facial expression whatsoever, not if he's made money or if he's lost it. He's older than Saki by a dozen or so years and stoop-shouldered and hobbled-up-looking and, to my observation, never happy. He never laughs, never looks you in the eye. It's hard to believe he's Saki's brother.

Because Saki, he's always laughing, always smiling, even if something bad happens. Like if a couple of teenage kids try shoplifting a couple of T-shirts or somebody crashes on group ride or *Saki* crashes out mountain biking or he eats too much at the Great Wall buffet last night. You name it, and somehow Saki will find occasion to smile about it. He'll laugh his high-pitched ha-ha laugh and slap a hand to his knee and say, "Too much Great Wall last night: give me the shits this morning. But I'm okay now. Group ride tonight gonna be *good.*"

That's an excellent way to stay healthy, by the way: Be happy. Find the humor in things. Don't take yourself too seriously. Be cool with life.

Saki *is* happy. He's what I'll always think of when I think of *happy.*

He's at the shop six days a week, from ten in the morning till five-thirty in the evening. As much as Saki works, as much as he's involved with bicycles, I'm surprised he doesn't say, *This bike shop too much, I need a long break.*

But no. He's positive all the time.

After the shop closes, he goes on group ride Mondays and Wednesdays and Fridays during daylight savings time, in all imaginable weather, thunderstorms, cold rains, brutal heat, et cetera. Saki *never* misses group ride, he can't, it's *his* ride, he is the *ride leader,* he recruits the people, sets the routes, holds the group together. Since there's never a group ride when at least a few people don't show up, Saki always has to go.

The rest of the year, during standard time, people come on Mondays and Wednesdays and Fridays to ride trainers after the shop closes. This isn't as popular an activity as the outdoor group ride. I mean, it's not everyone who can sit on a bicycle, indoors, for *two hours*, and do, for instance, after a ten-minute warmup, twenty minutes of alternating one-leg drills, then a twenty-minute out-of-the-saddle steady-state interval, followed by sprint intervals and various climb progressions and surge progressions and other periods of hurt that go nowhere, that's right, because the only reward you get from riding indoors, I swear to God, is the relief you feel when it's finally over. Many trainer nights, Saki and me *are* the group, we're *it*, but there you go: I'm there, Saki can't take the night off.

There's something wrong with both of us, no doubt about that.

But look at the bright side: Saki's bought a nice new Sony TV and has amassed an extensive library of bike-race videos, and while we're suffering on the trainers we watch tapes of Lance in various Tours de France, or we watch other races, the 1997 Milan–San Remo or the 2001 Tour of Flanders or the 1999 Paris–Roubaix or *The Fausto Coppi Story* or a variety pack of the finest Giri d'Italia and Vueltas d'España, you've got to admit the videos are cool.

So Saki usually doesn't get back home every evening till nine o'clock. Makes for a long day.

For Sausaiuda, too, Saki's wife. A long day for her. She arrives at the shop with him in the morning and doesn't go home till he goes. Oh, and the two parrots making all that racket in the back room, those two conures, they're Sausaiuda's. She walks around the shop with one or both of them on her shoulder, talking to them in Thai, trying to calm them when they screech and carry on.

Sausaiuda's a lot like Saki, happy all the time, laughing, having a good time at the shop. She graduated not too long ago from SIU, with a degree in education and teaching English as a second language, but she's working at the shop for now, keeping the books. She's known Saki for more than forty years, since they were children in a small village in Thailand. She likes children, always makes a big fuss when children come in, but doesn't have any of her own. The regular customers, friends of Saki's, et al., when they stop in she's completely excited to see them, as it's been *months* since the last time, even though it's usually just a couple of days. She gets so excited she startles the parrots, who go crazy all over again and screech and carry on.

So when you come in the shop you have Saki and Sausaiuda at the front counter yelling *Hello* and the parrots are going berserk, squawking their feathers off, and on the TV, with the volume way up, you have Phil Liggett and Paul Sherwin commenting on some bike race or other. Go in the back room, the repair area, and you have a top-quality eighties-era Yamaha stereo system, four speakers, cranking out Zeppelin, Hendrix, Sabbath, Deep Purple, Dio, Floyd. The good stuff. The shop is a grand crazyhouse of noise.

# HEFT ON WHEELS

Sausaiuda calls me Doctor Mike, because I'm a professor, even though I'm not a doctor. I'm a Mister. But why correct her? Doctor Mike's cool with me. Just let me keep hanging out *here*.

The ponytailed Thai fellow wearing the ball cap and the flannel shirt that's two sizes too big, that guy putting a new chain on a BMX bike, that's Choak Samkroot. He's here at the shop six days a week, too, and does the workhorse load of the mechanical repair in the back. Choak is not, contrary to various customer opinions, Saki and Sausaiuda's cousin or son or brother or anything like that at all. No relation. Except that he's Thai. He's thirty-eight years old now and arrived here in Carbondale from Thailand when he was twelve and his parents were here at SIU getting PhDs in Agriculture or Economics or I don't know what. Nobody seems to know. Some subject, anyway, and to get a PhD in *any* subject—it ain't easy. You could forget your children in the process, which was what Choak's parents did. They forgot him.

He never picked up English too great but he did pick up a BMX bike and started beating around town with the other jean-jacket BMX types, Saki being one of them, and of course, to go along with the BMX, plenty of smoking and drinking and getting rowdy and truant and being about as delinquent as a teenager can be, short of actually getting sent to reform school. Choak's parents couldn't handle him, in a word, and when they received their PhDs in a couple of years, they returned to Thailand and left Choak here in

Carbondale. Saki, who was seventeen at the time, took Choak in and has taken care of him ever since. Saki's older brother had a bike shop; at least they could get jobs *there* and make enough money to eat.

That guy in the back of the shop, rifling through Choak's toolbox and munching on a cookie, that's Geoff of Geoff-and-Christina fame, the people with the tandem. Geoff is a bluegrass upright bass fiddle player, a really good one, plays for Carbondale's famous group Shady Mix, and he's a guy who likes to clown around and joke and ride bikes as much as possible. Him and Saki and Choak have been hanging out for more than twenty years. Geoff doesn't work at the shop, just brings in his assortment of thirty-year-old Italian friction-shifting bikes and tunes them up with Saki's tools. Saki doesn't mind that one bit. Saki likes it when Geoff hangs around. Saki always says his shop is a better place when his friends are here.

I've seen Carbondale Cycle on a Saturday at noon—only this July, for instance—with easily twenty-five people hanging out there: some customers browsing through bikes; three college-age guys from Virginia, with fully loaded touring bikes, panniers, the whole works, riding across America into the wind, from east to west!; some of Saki's old friends or former employees or friends from the community hanging out near the counter; four Thai people sitting around the table in back, and four hippie mountain-bike kids there next to them; everybody eating chips and salsa or cookies or fresh fruit or whatever else people have brought in. Children run loose in the shop, and the birds squawk, and Saki's got a VCR tape of this morning's Tour de France stage playing on the TV. All the hubbub here, folks laughing, enjoying themselves, healthy well-adjusted people who don't have bags under their eyes and heavy loads of depression in their hearts, this place, it's just so alive.

Saki says, *Ride together*.

Some days I feel I've biked myself into forever and ever amen, that my life and everything that flows from it has become the open road, the fresh air, the sun, the heat, the clouds, the rain, my feet spinning in perfect circles. I feel so much colder now, so much smaller. I feel like the road I'm floating over isn't even there.

My life itself, and I think about this every day, has wheels under it. Either I'm on a bicycle or thinking about cycling or thinking about what's become of me because of cycling this year, my greatest cycling year of all time, how cycling has allowed so many of my dreams to come true.

I weigh 185 pounds now, probably less. Probably 180. I haven't had a drink in months, since July 4—hasn't hardly even occurred to me that I've quit drinking, in fact, I've been so focused on the bike. And cigarettes, the way I think about them now, how revolting the stink is when someone lights up near me, man, how could I have smoked those in the first place?

My old life, the cigarettes, the tonnage, the cases of beer, all *that*. Thrown away. It's dead.

Do this. I'm serious. Turn yourself into a new person, lose the weight, discard the bad habits, totally succeed with all of this. Then, at your moment of success, look at yourself in the mirror and see if you can concentrate on *anything*. See if you can be rational. See if you won't, for weeks and weeks and weeks, go around telling yourself *My God, I did it, My God, I did it, My God, I did it*. Then, under these conditions, when you are babbling and overjoyed and incoherent with thrill, see if you can show up at your job and be effective there.

I'm teaching again, well into the fall semester now. I shouldn't be teaching. I should be at the very least in an outpatient rehab program. I mean it. That's how to do it, right? Ask for help?

Sure, everybody at school notices. How could they not? People tell me I still sound like me, but man, where did all that Magnuson go? On the smoking deck near the English department, last year, I stood for fifteen minutes an hour, smoking and shooting the breeze with my colleagues and my students—all those friends, all those pleasant conversations, all of it, gone. Goes without saying, too, that I'm gone from the bar, the action there, beers and shots and intense discussion of literature, the *real* intellectual action of the writing program.

An outsider. How the English professor in me loves *that!*

But it's true, I've become an outsider. Literally. I've spent so many afternoons outside these last many months I'm able to notice how the sunlight's slant is different every day of the year and how the shadows change in consequence and in turn how the same stretch of road, because of the varying light and shadow, will never look the same from day to day. In this way, the road is always new. I have no occasion to become bored with it. The air, I can feel its moisture or its lack of it, or whether the pressure is changing for the better or for the worse.

I ride with Darren more often now, afternoon after afternoon, out on the Wine Trail, the route Darren likes best because he stops at Von Jakob's Vineyard for a glass of white wine every ride. An odd thing, I know, a rider of his caliber having a glass of wine during every workout, but hey, I don't begrudge the guy his quirks. I've got no problem being his designated cyclist.

Nevertheless, the Wine Trail's road surface is about the worst there is around here, and that means it's horrendous at best, with sticks on the road and loose gravel in the blind corners and rocks and hickory nuts and osage oranges and potholes, and to ride on it means beating the crap out of ourselves, taking a major pounding, but that's cycling, I've found. At least if you're going to take up cycling in southern Illinois with Darren it is. Fridays, for relief, we ride on Route 3 by the Mississippi River, seventy miles, coming on fall now, into October, sometimes riding all afternoon in a fifty-degree driving rain, miserable conditions, but we keep riding, not hard, just riding somewhere, it doesn't matter where.

Saki says we never ride aimlessly. Saki says, *Just have fun out there.* Saki says, *Ride within yourself and you'll stay with the group every time.*

But all the time I've been getting faster, Saki's been getting slower and slower.

Saki's been losing weight, too.

Go to the shop some afternoon now. He's not there. He's at home, or if he's not at home, he's at the doctors in St. Louis, and if he's hearing positive news from those doctors, I would doubt it. He's got tumors in his liver, big ones, too big to be removed. Saki's dying. He'll never make it.

That's the way I think: He'll never make it. Here *I* have made it, definitely, made a lifetime dream come true, a miracle for me, and it's a miracle that Lance Armstrong, the hero of our sport, survived cancer, but Saki, he isn't going to have a miracle. He's probably been sick for a year and hasn't told anyone. Either that, or the medical treatment is so shitty in Carbondale that they never caught the cancer those five or six times when he was ravaged by diarrhea and went to Carbondale Clinic and they told him, *You'll be fine, Saki. You have the GI flu.* That's right, they told him he had the GI flu.

In early August he takes off his shirt and notices his liver is protruding from his belly. Goes to Carbondale Clinic then, and what do they tell him? He's got hepatitis

B. Yeah, that's it. He must have eaten some bad fish or rotten meat or contaminated vegetables or whatever; that stuff can give you hepatitis just the same way a needle can. Seems logical. And there's Saki, one of the healthiest-living people in Carbondale, with a disease intravenous drug users get. The doctors tell him to eat plenty of fruits and vegetables, take it easy, and you'll be fine, Saki.

He starts thinking, wait a second, I'm not going to be fine, I don't have hepatitis B, the doctors have to take another look at this, and they do, and this time they get the diagnosis correct: Liver cancer. Stage four.

In late October, just before daylight savings time comes to a close, a group ride is leaving from the Carbondale Cycle parking lot at quarter to six in the evening. It's not a very long ride, not enough light for it to be. Not worth showing up for, in point of fact, which I still can't get over that's what I think, that a twenty-three-mile ride just isn't enough, but that's the ride, that's our lives, we show up for group ride even if it's not long enough to give us the workout we need.

Only a few of us tonight. Don and me and Ed and so on. The hardcores. And Saki's in the shop, sitting on the bench by the door.

Of course he looks like hell: ashen skin, very gaunt, eyes withdrawn and sunken, a three-quarter-size wax mannequin of himself.

Don kneels in front of him and listens. Don's a

psychologist. He's very skilled at listening. Saki says something about wanting to fight it hard, like it's climbing the Smiley Face Hill from Makanda up to U.S. Highway 51, something that, with the proper attitude, can be overcome. He's got chemo the next few weeks, then a surgery, then some more chemo. After that, he says, he'll be back on the indoor trainer by December, maybe January at the latest, then back on group ride, strong, come spring. *Lance could do it,* Saki says.

I'll never remember the ride that follows, no matter how hard I try. It's a ride. Everything's a ride. Getting dark too soon outside, every day a little colder, it's almost time to quit.

November. Darren says there is no need to stop cycling. He's solved my problem, for once and for all: I've got the wrong clothes.

He writes me an e-mail and tells me I need to keep riding outside in the cold, all winter long, I am not allowed to quit for the winter. It's a matter of commitment *and* investment. I'll have to buck up and buy the proper equipment. I have no choice. He sends me a list of stuff I need, too, and places where I can order it online, on sale. About five hundred dollars' worth of variously weighted Italian tights and jerseys and vests and arm warmers and leg warmers and socks and booties and hats and gloves. And for God's sake, he says, buy the stuff in the proper size, you can't keep riding around forever in those baggy cycling clothes, you need clothes that fit, you take a size medium now.

Check it out. A cardinal rule of life: *Never ever tell a person with a history of weight problems that he's got the wrong clothes.*

I have traditionally taken a size XXL in my jerseys and shorts and tights and such, and I mean an *American* XXL, which is a lot bigger than an *Italian* XXL, and now Darren's telling me to order five hundred dollars' worth of Italian clothes in size M? Medium? Me? I tell him, with the prerequisite grim realism, What if I put the weight back on?

Darren won't hear about it. Just get the clothes, he says.

I tell him, What the hell do you know about weight problems, dude? You dig how tenuous this situation is? I mean, if I could drop eighty pounds in that short a time, I sure as hell could put it on again in that short a time. And I complain a bunch like what's worked for him doesn't mean it's what will work for me, because my whole physiological-mental makeup is so vastly different from a person's who has perennially been lean. And some other stuff like money's real tight right now, if I want to waste five hundred dollars—et cetera. In short, I whine.

I present this rule as a reminder, and a review from chapter ten, because for damn sure it's so hard to follow: *Don't be a whiner.*

Darren is a good teacher, though. I'll give him his due. He knows I'm serious about cycling, that it's no joke with me, and consequently, soon, I'll figure out on my own that

I need to get new cycling clothes. That's a sign of a good teacher, knowing that the ones who are *supposed* to figure it out will *always* figure it out. You can't *make* it happen for somebody else; they have to do it themselves.

Incidentally, I protest most every suggestion Darren makes, not intentionally, really. It's a matter of reflex. I am what teachers often are: a horrible student. I'm so used to giving instructions I don't know how to listen. I know I should but well, darn it all, I just don't *want* to. Okay?

Besides, nearly every one of Darren's suggestions involve me either (1) spending more money on equipment or (2) admitting I actually have committed to the cycling lifestyle being a *permanent change*, not merely a temporary period of awesome fitness on which, a couple of years later, when I'm fat and drunk again at the bar, I'll look back and feel sorry for myself for not keeping it up. Poor Mike. I get drunk again, and you can bet the pot I'll be saying Poor Mike within the first hour.

Anyway, November, forty-degree highs nowadays, that's some cold, cold, brrrr cold, buddy, if you're going to be riding bikes in it. But I don't buy the clothes. And the misery on the road, it's the all-time worst, and, as you know, I have been through considerable suffering during my tenure on bicycles. I keep going out there, it keeps getting worse, I keep feeling more broken down and, for lack of a better way to put it, more frozen down, I am freezing my ass off out there.

One day Darren shows up in my office at school and

tosses me a paper grocery sack full of winter cycling
clothes, his. He's going to Washington, D.C., for a few
days on some grant thing and won't be needing this stuff.

A rule for future reference: *If you can't walk a mile in
another man's shoes, you can certainly ride a few miles in his clothes.*

The next afternoon, one o'clock, thirty-five degrees,
cloudy, wind from the northwest at ten miles per hour, I've
got all the gear on—windproof bib tights, vest, windstop-
per jacket and hat, booties, the whole works. My whole
life, I have classified someone of Darren's stature as a little
guy. He is five feet eight and maybe, if he's eaten a lot,
weighs 160 pounds. But his clothes, maybe they're a tad
too tight but hardly; you don't want your cold-weather
cycling clothes to hang loose. So I guess I'm a little guy,
like a ninja maybe, what with the gloves and hat and all the
killer gear. They say if you met yourself on the street you
wouldn't know yourself. That's so true.

By the way, I'm not in the slightest way cold.

Round about Thanksgiving, Saki has an operation, over in
St. Louis. The idea the doctors have, he says, is to close off
the blood flow to each of the large tumors in his liver, then,
it follows, the tumors will stop growing. The idea, further,
is that if his body can withstand the operation, his body
might be able to withstand further chemo, and from what
I can gather, seems the doctors are saying chemo is
optional.

And if chemo is optional.

One day in late November, sunny, forty degrees, hardly a breeze, Darren and I are cruising the Wine Trail, usual route, usual effort. I'm toasty warm and feeling great. I've made a sound like a wallet and bought the gear, imagine that, exactly the same stuff Darren has, so here we are, two dorks out cycling in matching outfits, but who cares? It's just such a kick that we're still out cycling, in December, in total comfort. Gotta love modern equipment.

I'm telling Darren, Yeah, you were right all along.

And he's like, Well, what did you expect?

We complete the Wine Trail route to where we're cutting through a valley and over a hill to Von Jakob's Winery, where Darren can have his glass of Cave Creek White and me my can of Coke Classic. It's a civilized ritual in the midst of a bike ride, actually. Stopping in and taking a break and shooting the breeze with the winery people. Everybody's totally used to us riding through.

We're coming up the hill, and there's a silver car approaching, slowing down—it's Somchai's wife and Sausaiuda in the car, and they've got Saki in the back.

We can only see him for a minute because of the chill that comes in when he rolls the window down. He's wearing a hospital gown and covered with a blanket. Skeletal but smiling. He shows us a tube running into his stomach. Laughs vaguely about it. Says, "They hook me up to a machine."

I ask him, just to be conversational, not that there needs to be a reason, "What are you doing out here today?"

He says, "I just wanna see them hills. Get ready for spring."

A couple of days later, Darren and I ride past Saki's place. He lives on Church Camp Road, six miles south from campus, on the south edge of Union Hill, beyond the neighborhood where the better-to-do college professors live. A fairly large property, a solid acre with considerable lawn and a gravel driveway dropping away from the road and down to his pole barn that's literally full of motorcycles and old cars and motors and lawn and garden equipment. A humble, tiny house near the road. A simple life within. But then a big honking pole barn full of toys out back.

Classic. Saki's a real classic.

The house is one-story two-bedroom but with a full basement below, where he keeps tropical fish and has a three-season porch with a wooden Thai buttress spanning it, just like the one spanning the display cases at the shop. I've heard the motorcycle collection in his pole barn is magnificent, but I've just heard about them, never been in there to see them, so much of Saki I've never been in there to see.

For as long as I can remember riding in southern Illinois, going past his house has been a standard route to Makanda, to the infamous Smiley Face water tower alongside U.S.

Highway 51. Group ride has traditionally passed his house at least once a week. We've met here, I don't how many times, on Sunday mornings for long rides. When I first moved to town, in fact, when I was still trying to get myself rolling and keep myself rolling, I used to ride up here past Saki's house in the mornings, about a quarter to ten, and invariably I would see Saki and Sausaiuda driving toward Carbondale in their little brown pickup truck, and I would think, man, someday I'd like to be friends with those people.

This is a Tuesday, a few days before Saki resumes his chemo at Barnes Jewish Hospital in St. Louis. I believe they're taking him up Sunday night. Sunny day. As clear and cold as my head.

Darren and I turn off Church Camp onto Saki's gravel drive and unclip to a stop and lean our bikes against his maple, helmets off, gloves off, mount the decking, and Saki opens the door. He was watching us coming. He'd been sitting in his chair, under a blanket, looking out at the road and waiting for just this, for a couple of cyclists to stop by.

Saki asks us to come in, please, and sit down, and the voice sounds like him but man, where did all that Saki go? He looks like a little hunched-over old man I've never met in my life.

Darren keeps the conversation pointed toward the future. He's buying a fancy Italian bike frame and fork, a Moser, from a shop in Nashville, Tennessee, and wants Saki to build up the frame with full Campagnolo, deluxe everything, even carbon cranks, not to mention handmade wheels. That should keep you busy, Saki.

Saki says he's made way too many mistakes along the way. He drank a bunch of sugar-water stuff, early on in his sickness, to help his liver, and in fact it only made his liver worse. Literally fed the tumors, he says. And for years he's avoided alcohol and dieted carefully to get his weight down to 135 pounds, so that he'd be an efficient climber on group ride, and what he needs most right now is maybe twenty extra pounds of fat to burn. All wrong, all wrong.

Sausaiuda comes home, and she says, "Dr. Mike . . ." Happy to see us but wants us to go. Saki needs more rest.

He walks outside with us, Darren carrying on about how that new set of wheels, that's just what the bike needs, and Saki shivers violently.

Saki has always hated the cold.

A couple of weeks later, on December 15, a Sunday, we gather at Carbondale Cycle, twelve noon, for a short easy ride, no hammering, no attacking, everybody stays together. There's been snow recently but not much, a couple of inches a few days ago. The sky is exquisitely pale blue, not a lick of wind, forty-five degrees, air dry but for the snowmelt moisture, a sudden dull chill a cyclist might feel on the road, passing from the sun into the shade. Seventy-five of us have come to ride, more than on any group ride anyone can remember. Riders are here from St. Louis, from Chicago and Springfield, from Marion, Herrin,

Vienna, Harrisburg, Cobden, Anna, and Cape Girardeau. More towns than that. Lawyers, doctors, schoolteachers, professors, house painters, policemen, college students. Everyone's bundled up and not saying much. The cycling season, for most of the riders here, ended more than a month ago. Only the hardcores are willing to buy the clothes and stay out on the road. A few people admit they haven't been riding much, you know, that's really too bad, but maybe, if the winter stays mild or if this is the year finally to get serious about an indoor-trainer regimen, could be this year, if everything goes right.

Even Choak rides today, in jeans, a blue flannel shirt, earmuffs, gloves. It's been years since anybody actually has seen Choak riding a bicycle.

Such sunshine, such a group we have today.

The group leaves the parking lot and rolls unhurriedly over the famous Carbondale railroad tracks, where each evening at nine-thirty the train they call the *City of New Orleans* passes through, and we ride into campus and around the lake around campus, spots of snow in the woods, among the pines and the hickories, a sound of breathing, sniffing, coughing here and there among the riders, gears clicking, nylon jackets rubbing, tires crunching over roads sprayed with salt and cinders only a few days ago.

People will get flat tires today, no doubt about that. There will be mechanical breakdowns.

From campus we ride past the university's agricultural

acreage, past the swine center and the horse center and up the long rise through Union Hill, the standard route toward the Smiley Face water tower in Makanda. This time of year, it's almost the winter solstice, the sun so low on the southern horizon it feels like a large dim flashlight spreading its beam on the road, making the road seem to shine and disappear near the point from which the brightness comes. The riders and their bikes and their plastic helmets glare and sparkle and become indistinct the farther up the road the group stretches.

Dr. Fred, the oral surgeon, attacks off the front, gets ten, twenty, fifty, a hundred yards out, but nobody picks up the pace to catch him, he'll stay off the front, out there, disappearing into the glare, and I won't see him again for almost a month.

We ride two by two, easy stroke by easy stroke, climbing all together to the first ridge on Union Hill, five miles from town now, and descending and taking the short flat road to Church Camp, to Saki's house, where we roll to a stop.

His house is tiny and humble, with snowy patches in the front-yard shade, and shafts of dull sunlight through the pine boughs connect the sky with his deck. We stare at his front door for a very long time, a white rectangle shielding life from the elements that make it miserable. No one talks. No one here would know what to say. We wait for his door to open, and for his laugh and his smile to follow, but it does not open.

# 13

One of my many failures in life is that I haven't turned out to be the teacher I once upon a time hoped I would be. When I first started teaching, when I was thirty, teaching English 101 at Mankato State University, I was just so darned enthusiastic it would nauseate you, just to hear me talk back then. Saying I would cut no corners, I would devote full attention to every student and to every word the student produced on the page, I would make my course *the* definitive, comprehensive, encyclopedic approach to the five-paragraph essay, sure, stressing that *this material* was something sacred I was imparting upon them, a gift they could use for the rest of their lives, a love of English Composition.

*If you love English Composition,* I used to say, *it will love you in return.*

Think about that next time you write a memo at work. Seriously.

These days, ten years of teaching later and God only knows how many thousands of students I've taught and how many hundreds of thousands of pages of student material I've marked up, well, let's just say my enthusiasm has waned somewhat. I've lost a step or two, or *it* has, the subject of English Composition, or I've discovered that the more you put into it doesn't necessarily mean the more you are going to get out of it.

A student might write me a few paragraphs, and it's highly probable, I kid you not, that *every word* in those paragraphs will be flawed in some way and in need of a rewrite. And I can point this out to the student. I can circle all the mistakes and write mean comments in the margins like *Look how wrong this all is, what were you thinking, how you could hand in such junk?*

I can make students cry when I teach in this manner, but I realize now I've never taught them anything by making them cry.

Does it really matter, for example, if a kid consistently misuses the semicolon if he doesn't understand what I'm telling him when I say, *Kid, first thing you have to do to succeed is sacrifice?*

This is how I teach these days. I say, *Try as hard as you can.* I say, *Take pride in what you're doing.* I say, *Find joy in your work.*

Some of my students get it. I can see the electrical circuits completing in their heads, and what happens is they go home at night and *study*, or they take long walks and contemplate what they've been studying, and in turn, if everything works out correctly, which in one out of every couple hundred students it does, they develop an obsession for the subject, and all the myriad little technical details involved in it make themselves evident. Not by accident. An obsessed person will by definition seek out little technical details and memorize them and review them at great length and put them to use.

Some of my students, especially my graduate students, think I'm a buffoon. They believe (1) I vastly oversimplify and perhaps trivialize things or (2) I've got limited talent in the first place, meaning my class is essentially worthless because I don't have a clue what it takes to be a top professional because I've never been a top professional myself or (3) now that I have tenure and such, I don't care enough to send my very best, buddy.

I hate it when I hear stories of grad students making such conjecture concerning me, but I'm sure they're making valid points. Graduate students always are, they'll tell you.

I used to send my very best. Just didn't do any good. Nobody got anywhere. Nobody learned anything worth

learning. I would yell and make scenes and scare a few students into writing the way I *told* them they should write,
but that's not learning, that's me burdening them with my
problems. Therefore, my very best—all that ranting and
raving and insisting everything's wrong, wrong, wrong—it
was bad acid, is what it was.

Now I'm teaching like cool, this is very cool work
you're doing, you've got tremendous potential, you can
succeed at this if you take this very seriously and put in the
time required to make yourself good.

One of the key things I ask of my students now is that
they open their hearts.

That's exactly how I say it to them, like a priest would:
*Open your hearts*. And I leave it at that.

I don't say, as I used to say, that in order to open your
heart properly, you need to perform a series of exercises in
the various aspects of heart opening.

I used to say, *Sit down and write a list of emotions that might
occur to a person who has just experienced a devastating loss. Take this
list then, and write down a physical object for each emotion connected
to the loss. Then take these objects, however many of them there are, and
a blank page, and use these objects to freewrite everything that crosses
your mind, what an awesome guy he was, how his favorite rides were
the hilliest rides, how his door won't open, how much you miss him and
can't bear it that you'll never see him again.*

I'd never tell my students to do that now. I couldn't do
it to them. There is no list of words or any sequence of
techniques that can combine to equal a human life.

*Carry on*, I tell my students.

I say, *Live a disciplined life.*

I make it through the holidays without drinking.

Close call there on New Year's Eve. About seven o'clock that night I nearly crack and just about get in the car and cruise to the liquor store for a case of Budweiser and a bottle of Jim Beam and some champagne and what else? Oh for sure a few bottles of twelve-dollar Chianti to aid the gourmet-hors-d'oeuvre digestion. Which means a trip as well to the grocery store to get heaps and heaps of stuff to make gourmet hors d'oeuvres. I want to chow down *heavily* on some hors d'oeuvres.

New Year's. Man, that's always been my top favorite of the annual stay-at-home drunks, right up there with the Fourth of July, that's one of the big ones, too. Thanksgiving, Easter, Memorial Day, Labor Day, those also are exceptional days for this type of drinking. Or you can be creative with this as well. You can have a party like this, on any night you want, for no particular reason!

Stay home, it's great. Lay in party supplies, and we're talking *enough*, meaning at *least* a twelve- or eighteen-pack more than you think you need, same with all other necessaries, cheese dip, olives, pretzels, chips, gourmet hors d'oeuvres, and so on. The idea is unlimited supply, tremendous bounty, so when you pass out in a stupor near dawn you're ending on a happy note, there's beer still in the fridge, which means the party *could* have kept going, which isn't the same as oh, dude, the beer's run out, we've eaten all the chips, what a drag, see you some other time maybe.

Moreover, a planned stay-at-home drunk is without question the most responsible form of heavy drinking there is, don't you agree? Think of the safety, holing up with a killer supply of booze and eats and being able to get as bombed as possible without ever having to get in a car and drive. No driving, no potential accidents or DUI problems or anything.

I say all this to my wife, too, on New Year's Eve. I say, Dammit, I'm gonna go to the store and get a load and come back here and get a load *on*.

And she's like, Well, if that's what you want to do, it's your decision.

She's been around me for a long time, she knows the rule: *You can't stop Mike from drinking, if that's what he wants to do is drink.*

Maybe precisely because my wife says go ahead, you make the choice, Mike, maybe I'm like wait a second, I've sacrificed and suffered and waded through a thick swampload of crap to come this far, I'm not going to break down now and blow it just because wow, this is New Year's Eve, this is the holiday designated the world over for epic drinking. I mean, I don't have to drink just because someone *says* I'm supposed to.

A close call. No doubt about it. But I don't crack. I go to bed when the kids go to bed, late for them, around nine-thirty, and fall directly to sleep.

The next morning, as you might imagine, is incredible. I feel fantastic. I would go so far as to describe my attitude and my physical state as *chipper*.

This is the first New Year's Day in twenty-two years I haven't been blindly hung over, barely able to get off the couch, sick to my stomach, and sick at heart.

Now I'm *chipper*. A couple of years ago, who'da thunk it?

At noon the temperature is forty degrees, windy and gray and threatening to spit snow, and Gerald and Don and me and a couple other folks, we get out and roll forty-five miles around the lakes and through Giant City Park and up the Smiley Face Hill out of Makanda up to Highway 51. We don't push too hard, but we don't go too slow. Just fast enough to stay warm.

Gerald keeps saying he feels *great*. He's made a point of going for a long bike ride every New Year's Day since he quit drinking. Don't matter the weather, Gerald's out there in it, he feels great, he's telling everybody he feels great. He's healthy and physically fit and tough enough to suit up and grind out forty-five miles on a forty-degree day. Many years in a row he's been out here on New Year's Day. And why wouldn't he feel great? He didn't do anything stupid last night. He went to bed at ten.

I should tell my students I'm jerking their chains. When I say one thing to them, I usually mean another. I am not lying to them, not exactly, but if I'm attempting to tell them something true, because I don't really mean what I'm saying, I really mean something *else*, I end up offering a generalized, maybe-not-totally-true version of the truth, an incomplete version of it.

Like I tell my students my wife bought me a gymnasium-quality stability ball a couple of months ago.

*My* wife, I say, gets me a stability ball. She thinks that's something I could *use*. A stability ball.

And the students laugh.

And I say I've named my stability ball Gertrude and every morning at six o'clock, for approximately twenty minutes, I roll around on top of Gertrude and contort myself into positions both obscene and unseen, and the wife's *cool* with this. She says, That's fine with me, Mike. Roll around on Gertrude all you want.

My favorite ball routine—wait, did I just say *ball routine?*—is the ball crunch—did I just say *ball crunch?* I mean, I believe in no-pain-no-gain but how much pain are we talking about here?

And the students laugh some more.

But then I'm serious with them. Bring the tone down, soften up the presentation, look them in the eye. Say I'm honestly doing 120 ball crunches a day, six days a week, the idea being to increase my core strength and thereby improve my bike-handling skills and my balance and reduce the possibility of back injury, and by adding five more crunches every week, I'm hoping to build up to the number of daily ball crunches that Britney Spears does, 350.

Britney Spears: 350 ball crunches a day. That's bad *ass*. She's *tough*. She's got my *complete* respect. If I can train myself to become as tough as her—and that's the great thing about it, I can—I'll have gotten somewhere. And you, if you apply yourself, can get somewhere, too.

End of lesson and serious tone.

And my students, I pray to God, will have learned something.

They usually laugh, or *have* laughed somewhere along the line, and we move on.

See, I don't know how many ball crunches Britney does or even if she does them at all. I totally don't care, matter of fact. I'm sure she works hard, though. You don't get to become an intense worldwide superstar like Britney if you don't work really, really hard.

Truth is, I've never had it in me to work as hard in life as Britney does, which is why I'm not an intense worldwide anything. I am a humble English professor at a humble university in a humble part of America.

Truth is, my life hurts, everybody's life hurts, I want my students to know that, but that's not what I tell them. I make fun of the ways I'm trying to hurt myself instead.

Out riding, we don't talk about Saki, not for a while. We talk about how horrible the riding conditions have become. Seems like once a week we have snow, not heavy snow like the kind of snow that fell when I was a boy in Wisconsin, but snow enough to shut down the roads, to limit the places we can ride. Back in Wisconsin, too, the county highway crews have the equipment and the know-how to rid the roads quickly of snow, when to salt, when to plow, *how* to plow. This far south, not to fault anybody, but there just isn't the same level of experience with harsh winter conditions. Snow falls, people freak and either drive at a terrified two miles per hour or simply hole up in their homes and wait for the snow to melt, and the highway crews creep through the backroads spreading tons and tons of cinders. If the snow exceeds three inches, the highway crews try their luck plowing it, but because the roads are essentially gravel and tar, the plow blades will gouge enormous ruts in the road.

We have a vast supply of cinders, incidentally, in southern Illinois. Cinders are a byproduct of trash, of garbage, they are literally what's left over when you burn vast quantities of trash, they are the sludge at the incinerator's bottom. What do you do with them? Spread them all over the road when it snows.

One of the many ironies in this, the snow usually won't stick more than a day or two, and typically the snow will begin melting on the road as soon as it falls. For us lowly cyclists, the irony is compounded by the fact that cinders literally have the texture of finely ground glass, and if you've ever ridden a bike three hours a day on finely ground glass—right, you get the idea. Cinders are horrible on the tires, chewing them into a Swiss cheese in a matter of three hundred miles, and no matter what we do to prevent flat tires—using Mr Tuffy tire liners, buying fresh tires every three weeks—someone among us will get a flat on practically every ride. Outside, with a flat tire, at thirty-three degrees, windy, sleet falling, or even without a flat tire, just pedaling, just slicing through the wind when it's so cold outside our water bottles freeze rock-hard before we've barely gotten beyond the city limits, it's hard to maintain a good attitude.

But we go and go and go.

I tell my students that this is what you will face, hardship and misery and drudgery. If you think it won't involve all that, you are sorely mistaken, nothing will become of you.

Some days I wonder what's become of me.

Monday and Wednesday evenings now, till spring, I'm training indoors at Great Shapes Fitness Center for Women. Yes, it's true, I've become a Fitness Center for Women type of guy. But hey, we're going in there at night, Ed, Don, Geoff, Christina, during the gym's coed hours, and setting up our trainers in front of a floor-to-ceiling mirror. We stack some step-aerobic platforms and put a TV-VCR combo on top, pop in a Spinervals tape, turn up the volume, and *voilà*, we're sitting and spinning.

We have Dr. Fred to thank for these Spinervals

because he bought the whole series of nine, after which time, to give you an idea how rough Spinervals are, he hurt his back doing Spinervals with us at Great Shapes, so Fred won't be joining us. Actually, Fred won't be able to ride an upright bike ever again, he says. He'll be on a recumbent from now on, if he can ride at all.

Darren says Spinervals are too hard. And if they're too hard for Darren, let me assure you, they're too hard.

If you're not seriously into bike training, you won't know about Spinervals, and if you do Spinervals regularly, you're not likely to mention the fact to any of your noncycling friends because Spinervals, done properly, are not only ridiculously difficult but they're a bit embarrassing, featuring extensive close-up footage of people cycling, in place, under heavy loads—add this to the synthesizer soft rock in the background and the soft light and the undulate nature of the cycling motion, well, you get the picture. It's a private matter.

A Spinervals tape runs anywhere from forty-five minutes of "Suffer-O-Rama" to "Have Mercy: 120 Minutes of Suffering" and features the pleasant Coach Troy, his stopwatch, and sixteen male and female cycling gorillas set up in a semicircle and sweating and grimacing through their anaerobic thresholds into certain madness. Coach Troy leads the cyclists through a series of massive-effort interval bursts with names like *super spins, ladders, acceleration sets, spinsets*, his goal being to help "the serious cyclist learn how to tolerate discomfort" by going "through a series of steady state intervals increasing your threshold for discomfort and pain."

So Coach Troy says that the serious cyclist must learn how to tolerate discomfort. My days and weeks, all of it, my life, it's centered on accomplishing that goal, every moment, every morsel of food, how many minutes in the day I can spend being nice to my wife and kids, how many hours of sleep, hours on the bike, hours working, et cetera. I've got ambitions again, that's the problem. I have indeed achieved much on the bicycle, but I know I can achieve more. I know I can continue improving, meaning I keep trying to expand the difficulty, to do something harder, more challenging, humbling, self-mangling.

I don't eat much anymore. Get up in the morning, bam, I Osterize myself a shake with nonfat yogurt and skim milk and some peanut butter and protein powder and honey and a Granny Smith apple and a banana. Five hundred fifty calories. Next five hours, one pot of coffee, black, half a gallon of water, tap. For lunch, maybe another shake, maybe a small can of tuna and an apple. For dinner, sometimes a lot of food, really, nearly a pound of pork loin or a big steak with vegetables or a whole baked chicken. But never a potato, never a piece of bread, never any pasta, never any rice. Is this somebody else's diet? Like a famous one or something? I haven't read the book, in any case. I haven't read any book on the subject of dieting, actually. I'm improvising, guesstimating what others do and what might be physiologically wrong with me, what has caused me to be overweight my whole life.

When I was three and four and five years old, I had a disease called celiac, which is an intolerance to gluten, to wheat. I don't recall the symptoms, nobody in my family has ever spoken of them. I only know that the doctors put me on an extremely restricted diet, and photographs of me during this restricted-diet period reveal that the little Mikey was indeed a *little* Mikey, a lean Mikey, not a blobulent Mikey. When I was six, I was released from my diet and in every photograph thereafter, until just this year, I am most definitely big Mikey, he likes it, he'll eat anything.

So I'm thinking I'm not eating gluten now, maybe that's the reason I've lost the weight. Beer's got a lot of gluten in it, right? Got rid of that. And bread's got gluten. And pasta. And a bunch of other stuff, even soy sauce contains gluten, which surprises me somehow. And potatoes and rice, they don't have any gluten in *them*, but just to stay on the safe side, I'm not eating any.

I've taken out the calendar for the upcoming bicycle season, not the season I'm in now, which is the off-season that's really, in terms of brutal training, the *on*-season, but the season where legitimate events take place on the weekends, and I've marked down a variety of difficulty events. I'm thinking for sure I'd like to ride, in May, a couple of weeks after I turn forty, in the Assault on Mount Mitchell, an event in North Carolina that's basically like the Bridge to Bridge but with an additional four thousand feet of climbing over the same distance, and, four days *before* I turn forty, there's the 3 State 3 Mountain Challenge in Chattanooga, Tennessee, which looks on paper to be a hard hundred miles as well. Darren's been after me to try road racing, too, which to his face I keep saying no way, dude, that sounds too dangerous, too scary, but deep down I'm steeling up the nerve to join Darren's team and jump into a bunch of road races.

And why not? Why wouldn't I plan for an ambitious season? Why wouldn't I keep trying harder and harder and harder? What else am I gonna do? If the tavern's out of the question, if the sitting-around-and-smoking-cigarettes-with-my-intellectual-associates is out of the question, hell, I don't know anymore. It's too late, I believe, I've invested too much time on the bike, I believe, to do anything with the sport but set my sights higher and higher.

So I rise every morning before dawn and do ball crunches while the coffee's brewing: 125 ball crunches; 130 ball crunches; 135 ball crunches; 140 ball crunches. In forty-three weeks, progressing at this rate of five, I'll be doing 350 ball crunches a day. The crunches don't hurt as much as other forms of torture I've been enjoying of late, but they hurt a lot, not a stinging pain but a pressure type of hurt, like I've lost all this weight and what's left inside wants to burst free. Whenever I'm done with the ball, I stand up and say, "I'm killing myself here."

I work for a couple of hours then, sit at my desk and

mark up student writing. I try to be encouraging and help-ful and all that hocus-pocus I'm not as good at as I used to be. Or if I'm not marking up student writing, I sit in my easy chair and read novels, which may not sound like work to you but for me, an English professor—you're right, let's not go there. Some days it occurs to me that I haven't writ-ten hardly anything but e-mails since I quit smoking. Kind of like a switch turning off: quit smoking, bam, no interest in writing whatsoever. But I'm not alarmed. If God wants me to keep on writing, I expect He'll let me do it without a cigarette hanging from my lips.

Sometimes I skip lunch and spend the afternoon at the university hungry, on the edge of crazy, near to the point where I'm your basic Professor Renfield type sitting in my office muttering *Blood is the life, blood is the life*. When it's time for me to teach, I'll wander beforehand to the Student Center and get a quadruple espresso with lots of sugar—this on a very very empty stomach—and when I arrive minutes later in the classroom, I literally am a madman, talking way too fast, running around the classroom, mov-ing from this subject to that subject with blazing and prob-ably incomprehensible speed. My students seem to enjoy themselves, though. They generally spend most of the hour laughing; sometimes students will even tell me I should do stand-up comedy because I'm so insane and so all over the place. But I'm not doing stand-up, I say. I'm trying to teach you something. I want you to enjoy this subject.

# HEFT ON WHEELS

I never tell my students I think I'm crazy, but I do, I think I'm crazy.

On the afternoons I don't teach, I don't bother going to the university at all, and suit up in my layers of winter cycling clothes and hit the road and, while I'm shivering, dream of good times, maybe sitting in front the TV with a glass of beer and a large roast beef sandwich and a bowl of potato chips and not a single care in the world. But that's okay, I keep reminding myself. I've had my glasses of beer and roast beef sandwiches and good times. I don't need any more of that. Or maybe I do, I don't know anymore.

During Spinervals, when Coach Troy shouts out that we must click into our biggest gear and sprint, give one-hundred-percent effort, this is the highlight of pain for the week, blurring agony, the kind that sours the stomach and numbs the limbs and nearly bursts the aging heart. I've never met Coach Troy, only seen him on his tapes, but I believe he's hurting us to help us. We don't have to be here doing this. No way. We come. He instructs us to suffer. We suffer. And we become stronger.

Late February, February 21, a Friday afternoon, Don and Darren and I ride the usual Lick Creek route circling back into Cobden. We're looking at sixty-five miles with lots of hills but no aggressive riding. I can tell you unequivocally that this is my favorite type of ride: mellow and friendly. Temps aren't bad. Upper forties, lower fifties. Temps like these, after having slogged around for six weeks in the lower thirties, feel like a warm day. The sky is coated with thin yellowish clouds, and there's snow in the woods but none on the road, just the black lining of cinders and the new potholes everywhere. You about couldn't ask for a nicer day, I guess, except maybe if it were sunny and eighty degrees and if we had nice asphalt roads with the proper pitch and camber and things.

We're riding three-up along the road—hardly any traffic ever, midafternoon in the southern Illinois country-side—and hashing through our usual set of subjects: how superior we are to certain of our sedentary university colleagues, who, at this very instant, on a Friday afternoon, are sitting in their offices writing e-mails to each other or preparing to go to a wine-and-cheese reception at four or a cocktail party at five or a dinner party at six or whatever; or we talk about equipment, about fitness, about other cyclists we know.

Fact of it, today, I'm exceptionally chatty and excited because, by some miracle, even though I hardly write any-more and feel a bit like I'm in retirement from the disci-pline, I've got a writing gig coming up in a few weeks with *Bicycling* magazine, to travel to California and ride in the wine country north of San Francisco. I'm getting a fancy Litespeed titanium bike to use for the article, and I'll be staying in some fancy hotels and riding on some of the finest cycling roads in America. Apparently they have real asphalt out there in California.

# 14

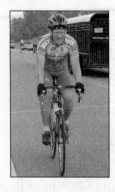

 

So we're talking and riding and moving along nicely, and I'm saying stuff like California's where the pros are, and Wow, it's supposed to be really killer riding out there, and Isn't it like winning the lottery that I'm gonna get paid to go biking?

We head south on a sleepy back road called Wolf Creek Road, which announces itself with a yellow highway sign that says HILLY TERRAIN. And we grind over the cinders over the hills—big rollers, very steep—and near the top of one of the hills, I feel something weird in my stomach, a quick knifing pain that comes and goes, but it's so severe I let out a holler.

Don's like What's up? You okay? And I'm like Nothing, nothing.

The point of cycling is pain, isn't it? So if you feel a sudden knifing pain, what do you do? Deal with it, buddy.

We ride over some more hills, and, because this is the way good cycling should be, we ride over more hills after that. Near the crest of each, though, my gut seizes up, a suckerpunch-to-the-midsection type of thing, and it's bad, it's getting worse, but I'm not going to yelp anymore. I'm sucking it up, I'm handling it, I'm trying to do what Coach Troy would want me to do, increase my ability to suffer.

But eventually, when we get to within a mile or two of the little town of Cobden, which has a gas station where we've been stopping for fluids for as long as I can recall riding in southern Illinois, I can't take it anymore. I can hardly stay bent over the handlebars, the pain in my guts is so intense. I can hardly breathe. Something major, I'm certain of it, is going wrong with me.

I say it, too, I admit it. "Something's wrong with me, guys."

"No kidding," Darren says. "You've been groaning for the last hour."

"I mean seriously," I say. "We gotta get me off the road."

I think I black out for a while in there, the pain in my guts is so gruesome, but I manage to ride all the way to the gas station, and Darren and Don get me inside, call my wife and tell her she's got to come and pick me up, but it's going to take a while for her to get here; Carbondale is six-teen miles from here.

Meantime, the woman behind the counter at the gas station has seen us lots of times and is totally cool about letting me stretch out on the floor, and while I writhe there on the cold linoleum, I feel like everything I've done in the name of good is finally collapsing around me. Darren's say-ing something like I've got appendicitis for sure, that takes months to get over. And I'm saying Dammit, I'm going to California in three weeks, ain't nothing gonna stop me. Darren's like No way, you're hurt, you need help. And I'm envisioning my recovery period from my appendectomy, the doing-nothing period, the logical extension of which will be drinking and therefore smoking and therefore weight gain and therefore unhappiness and, Coach Troy, dude, what do you want me to do?

About an hour later, at the Urgent Care Center at the Carbondale Clinic, a doctor is examining me, asking me questions about what I've been doing, how much I've been exercising, my relationship with Gertrude, and so on, and he doesn't look too worried.

He says, "You know what's wrong with you, Mike?"

I'm like, What is it? Is my appendix fried?

"No," he says. "You need something to eat."

**14**

Three weeks later, several billion wonderful calories later, I'm experiencing a state of uninterrupted ecstasy. I am, using legal and available-at-your-supermarket substances, freaking out. I'm *eating*. And I flat-out can't believe how much my life has improved since I've begun eating again. I am *so* much happier. I have *double* the energy, *half* the aches and pains. I can concentrate for longer periods of time. I am ten times as strong on the bike as I was only one month ago. I kid you not. Remember that part in *Barfly* when Mickey Rourke finally gets something to eat— bread and cheese and meat and a few bottles of ___

wine—and he shows back up at the bar with a "full tank of fuel" and ready to beat the crap out of Eddie?

That's me. I've got a full tank of fuel—minus the wine, anyway. I don't know why this seems so miraculous to me right now, but wow, food's the answer. Food's really some amazing stuff, isn't it?

I am so excited and stunned that I hereby declare the key rule for maintaining an athletic lifestyle is this: *Eat, eat, eat.* You have to *eat.* You have to take in huge loads of fuel if you're going to expend huge stores of energy.

Check out the load I've taken on in the last thirty hours, traveling from Carbondale to northern California and getting set up for that first killer 110-mile riding day I have planned:

At the Denver airport, I get the large fish burrito, which my guess is at least 1,200 calories large, maybe more, and no other way to say it, it's great, it's fantastic. I don't care what you tell me otherwise, the Denver airport's got the best burrito stand in the world. I should have eaten two.

I get to California, rent a car, and drive north from San Francisco to the little town of Healdsburg, which is north of Napa Valley a piece, and I check into my hotel and drive to this place called Big John's Market to get a stockpile of fuel. I'll admit it, I'm a midwestern boy used to buying produce and deli items at Wal-Mart Super Center, I'm not very civilized, so when I'm seeing all this gourmet ultragreat food for sale at Big John's Market, I'm hard-pressed not to buy it all.

I end up getting two massive trays of sushi rolls because I've never seen sushi rolls in a grocery store and why not? When in Rome, right? And I get a pint of fresh guacamole and a huge bag of organic tortilla chips and a pint of artichoke/cheese/jalapeno dip and several pieces of fresh fruit, and I book into my hotel, turn on the TV, and hit the feedbag hard.

Let me assure you, folks, one hour later, not one crumb of this stuff remains.

Talk about fueling up for the ride, hey?

I'm a happy guy.

When in Rome. In the morning, when I'm getting ready to go riding—*have another bagel, Mike, you'll need it, and drink some more water while you're at it*—I stand outside my hotel door, a place called the Madrona Manor, an extremely *yellow* and extremely *humongous* Victorian inn a mile west of Healds-burg, and survey the countryside. Everywhere, in the flats and on the hillsides and in town and in the country, the land is covered with grapevine, California wine country, and this time of year the vines aren't laden, it's not like a person can get a mere glimpse of the fields and catch a buzz, but, man, within a fifty-mile radius of where I'm standing, this is where all my favorite wines are made. When in Rome.

I don't know if I'm going to make it. Oh, for one tall glass of ice-cold California Chardonnay!

My magazine assignment is—you don't really care what it is, do you? I'm supposed to ride my bike, and that's all I need to know.

I saddle up and spin from Madrona Manor to the center of Healdsburg, to another magnificent market, the Oakville Market on the town square, where I'm going to meet up with a cyclist named Mark, who's going to show me the area and let me know what kind of riding's available, and go riding today from here over the mountains to the ocean and back. A classic ride, he's told me. We'll do a difficult portion of the famous Terrible Two Double Century, taking Skaggs Springs Road forty-eight miles over to Route 1 in Stewarts Point, then south to Fort Ross, and the legendary Fort Ross Road, apparently one of the toughest two-mile, 1,500-foot climbs a person could ever do. There's another forty miles to go after that, I guess, 110 miles or so today. Easily ten thousand feet of climbing. Ah, the pain. I'm going to *love* it.

Not a cloud in the sky today. Nine o'clock sharp on a Sunday morning, sixty-five degrees. The Healdsburg town square is nicely manicured, flowers in bloom, and watered and green, with fountains bubbling and brick walkways and clean benches and a white gazebo before which there's an open area for small concerts and other civilized gatherings and whatnot. Four handsome-looking white women have commandeered the gazebo this morning for t'ai chi, they move to the right and hold a pose and move to the left and hold a pose, very unified, very elegant, very cool, I'd like to try that t'ai chi stuff sometime, looks to be relaxing. Surrounding the gazebo, on the benches near the fountains and among the flowers and well-watered plants, are several dozen Mexican men, smoking cigarettes and pretending not to be watching the four white women and their outstretched arms, with their fluid changes from this position to that position, the healthy lives they're living, how they are unashamed to display their health and vitality in a public place.

I guess I'm watching the women, too—never seen people doing such a thing in the middle of town before—and even though I think it's cool what they're doing, I think it's a little weird, too. But hey, I'm a little weird-looking, all decked out in my cycling gear, $4,500 bike, shaved legs, and so on. Or at least I would be in southern Illinois. Hereabouts, no worries about being perceived as a freak. A cyclist is not out of place in California. There's so many cyclists in this part of the country, they're everywhere you look. Just yesterday afternoon, when I was driving north across the Golden Gate Bridge out of San Francisco, I could see on the pedestrian lanes a line of road cyclists stretching either way, as far as the eye could see. Hundreds and hundreds of cyclists. And they weren't participating in an organized event; they were just out riding. That's how many cyclists there are around here.

Mark shows up, riding no-handed, dressed in black, the epitome of style on a bicycle, and of course he's completely cool, and we ride off into the legendary cycling distance, where the hills are incredibly steep, and the road surface, wow, too much, too perfect.

I mostly hang in there, at least on the uphills, all day. The descents are twisty and scary and like nothing I'd ever imagined could exist, and Mark drops like a stone away from me, he's bombing so much faster than me. He says it's no biggie, though. I'll get used to it. In a few days, I'll bomb downhill twice as fast as I can now.

Mark's an excellent cyclist, and like every excellent cyclist I've encountered, he's a good conversationalist, because what else are we going to do for hours on end out there but *talk?*

It's a great sport. Like sitting at the bar, except without the bar and the booze.

He tells me the names of the trees we're passing, the madrones high up on the climbs, the redwoods in the lowlands, the eucalyptus near the ocean, and he sets the pace on the uphills, hard enough to hurt me but not enough to drop me, because he doesn't want to drop me, why would he? This isn't a race or a training ride or anything structurally useful whatsoever. We're just riding and seeing the sights.

At Stewarts Point, we stop at this frozen-in-time gas station by the sea, waves raging and rolling and smashing the rocks two hundred feet below the road.

A singular coastline, Mark says.

It certainly is. It's awesome. This is the greatest day of cycling I've had in my whole life.

Mark gets a couple of cans of Red Bull energy drink and a bag of Fritos, and I'm like, that looks good, I'll have some, too, and twenty minutes later, when we're climbing Fort Ross Road, fifteen hundred feet up from the ocean in two miles, and he's dropped me, and my guts are so torn up I'm about to barf, I'll have learned something, the *wrong* thing, but something nevertheless: *Don't drink Red Bull and eat Fritos during the greatest day of cycling you've had in your whole life.*

I recover, though, at the top of the hill, and ride forty more miles before getting back to the Madrona Manor, my hotel.

End of the day, I've ridden longer than I've ever gone at one time, 110 miles, and I'm worse than toasted. I'm completely blown.

After dark, after I've showered and changed, I'm seated for dinner downstairs in the Madrona Manor, and I'm feeling like the underground man in Dostoyevsky's *Notes from the Underground.* I am a sick man, I'm thinking. I'm wildly thirsty, mildly hysterical, hallucinating, sweating. I'm paranoid *because* I'm sweating. And what else? I'm insanely hungry.

Surrounding me: some other cyclists, fourteen casually dressed, perfectly well-mannered people seated at two long elegant dining tables in this room, which is very darkly lit by nineteenth century-style lamps, very mellow. These cyclists are on vacation with a company called Backroads; they're from all over the country, they've got their God-only-knows-what reasons for vacationing with Backroads. They're enjoying a few glasses of wine and talking about having trained for this trip, having taken the Spinning classes, three times a week, all winter, et cetera, and they're afraid of their first day of riding, tomorrow, expressing fears about the hills and the twenty-two miles before lunch. They're chitchatting, is all.

A hush in the room now, and waiters in crisp white uniforms maneuver themselves into view, meaning the grand rock opera of California fine dining is about to begin.

I consider applauding.

The man across the table from me says, just to make sure what I've been telling everybody for the last ten minutes is indeed true, "You rode a hundred and ten miles today."

I say, "Climbed ten thousand feet, too."

The waiters now bring bottles of Pellegrino to the table, swooping in with them, filling glasses. The ecstasy! What a grand substance bottled water is!

The man says, "And you're gonna ride like that all week?"

"Or till I drop," I say. "Whichever comes first."

I chug a full glass of water and fill myself another and oh, now the waiters are bringing out baskets of piping-hot homemade bread and, dude, what about this cloverleaf salad with marinated dates and blue-cheese crumbles the size of marbles? And ladies and gentlemen, here comes the totally stupendous bacon-wrapped filet mignon with four extrajumbo shrimps and a pan-seared root-vegetable cake presented with a sauce, dear Lord, the finest sauce—

The man across from me says, "Are you okay, Mike?"

I say, "I believe the chef deserves a Nobel Prize!"

The man says, "You're crazy."

Stephen. That's his name. He's one of the Backroads trip leaders, a laid-back guy, a handsome fellow, dark hair, clear-eyed, physically fit, about thirty years old, been a Backroads trip leader for a few years, pretty much finds good-natured amusement in everything, likes to crack jokes and make fun of himself. He was born and raised in Santa Rosa, not far from here, but with Backroads he's been all over the world. He says, "But you're right, Mike"—forks a piece of medium-rare filet and regards it the way an expert jeweler would a fine diamond—"the chef *rocks*."

"Telling you," I say, "I'm gonna quit my job in Illinois and spend the rest of my life climbing every killer climb and smoking through every killer loop I can find."

Stephen chews and nods in the affirmative, like *sure* you are, Mike.

One day. I've been out here riding one day—never once in my life set foot in California till yesterday—and these roads out here with the great asphalt, the mammoth coastal-mountain climbs and the funnest twisty mountain descents ever and plus with the godlike dining situation, man, one day's all I need to convince me: I'm packing up my family and moving to California. For real.

Just look at dessert: a caramel-filled chocolate brownie-slash-tart masterpiece served with homemade vanilla ice cream with, and it couldn't be any other way, a sprig of mint for garnish. I literally weep with every bite, and a compassionate lady from Florida notices my emotional bubbling-over and, in a tremendous act of human kindness and self-sacrifice, offers me her dessert, which I joyfully demolish in about thirty seconds flat.

"You can't run a horse," I say to her, "without food and water."

My mouth's full, though. I think she hears what I'm saying as a sort of primordial groan. She smiles anyway.

So I've ridden 110 miles today and trashed myself in the process. This is not proof of intelligence or clean living or systematic bicycle training, and it's not going to help me get respectable results in races or whatever my buddy Darren thinks cycling is all about, results in a race.

If I were doing the right thing, the intelligent thing, if I were to travel somewhere *else* in the country for a week, I should go to a real cycling training camp and have coaches prescribe me interval sequences and hook me up to a heart-rate monitor and probably discover that I'm legally dead. Ha!

See, I can't even talk seriously about it, I've got such a bad attitude.

Cycling is my *hobby*. Hobbies are supposed to be *fun*, not systematic forms of torture.

And that's the paradox of cycling. It *is* fun, but then again it isn't.

What about drinking? What about smoking? Where is the distinction? What is a life, now that we've broached the subject, but a series of happy moments punctuated by difficulties and unpleasantness?

Later that evening, in my room, I sit in bed and stare at the kickass bike I'm using this week and ask it for help. The bike's just as fabulous in person as you'd read about it in a catalog—a Litespeed Tuscany, silver and black and sleek and cagey, full Dura-Ace component gruppo, Ksyrium SSL SC wheels, seventeen pounds of Grade-A Upwardly Mobile Titanium—but the bike's got nothing to say. It's a bike.

I like the sound of this: Morning has broken. Sounds painful and at the same time beautiful. Sounds like I'm feeling, in fact. I've been stumbling around my room for an hour, hydrating and gathering my belongings and setting my suitcases outside my room door so the porters can pick them up and load them into the Backroads van, which will take my stuff to the next hotel down the road. When I wheel my Tuscany outside, wait, here's the Backroads trailer and next to it a table weighted down with heaps of M&M's and chocolate-covered raisins and granola bars and bananas and powdered Gatorade mix and gummy bears, looks like enough fuel for several pro teams for several very long stage races.

Jenny says, "They call it Snackroads." Then she looks at me sternly. "That means you, Mike. Eat." She's the other Backroads trip leader. She's roughly the same age as Stephen, is similarly fit and clear-eyed and easygoing, and to see her talking with the Backroads guests, fitness-minded professional people in their thirties and forties and fifties, it's obvious she digs people and thinks people are cool and wants to make sure they're having a good time.

Oh, and Jenny is like my grandmother, too. She never stops telling me eat, have some more, fuel up, one more brownie, don't hold back. She's actually giving me sound advice, too. I can't ride a hard hundred miles a day, six days in a row, without basically garbaging down everything edible that comes within reaching range.

So hey: I do what I'm told. No sense causing a ruckus.

I go to work on a whopping handful of M&M's while Jenny assembles everyone in front of a map and begins explaining today's variety of cycling routes, where lunch will be, where possible pickup points could be, where the big hill is, things to be careful of, things in which to find joy, all that.

The general drift of her remarks correctly paraphrases my plan for life.

# HEFT ON WHEELS

She says, *While you're here, you ride, you eat, you relax, you ride, you eat, you relax. The extent to which you pursue these options is your choice. You may do whatever turns your crank.*

All perfect.

We'll start from here in Healdsburg and then roll through valleys covered with grapevine the way Iowa is covered with cornfield: the Alexander Valley and into the Napa Valley and from there toward the ocean, to Sonoma and out to Bodega Bay, then back through the Russian River Valley and its monstrous redwoods to Healdsburg. Everywhere you go here you can park your bike outside the finest wineries in America and wander in for a taste. Robert Mondavi, Korbel, Sebastiani, Ernest and Julio Gallo; literally, you can name your favorite American wine, and you'll bike past its winery here, like cycling through the largest and most scenic liquor store in the world.

I'm beyond it, really. I don't need a glass of wine. I'm too happy, too *un*depressed, to need a glass of wine. That's why we have wine, right? To make things better? But I'm already better. I'm feel like I'm in heaven, and why would we need wine in heaven?

Another sunny day. A perfect life. *You need to believe this is possible.*

Seventy-two degrees, and the asphalt's wonderfully smooth, and I'm spinning fifty miles before lunch at the prearranged meeting point, a built-like-a-bunker-into-a-hill winery called Field Stone, where we picnic outside and chow down on pasta salad, macadamia nuts, a Caesar salad that breaks my heart, grapes, prosciutto, brownies, pecan/caramel bars—a five-star luncheon, no question about it.

Now the wind's at my back, and the road's downhill along the Silverado Trail all the way to Yountville in the heart of Napa Valley, forty miles away, and yes indeed I'm hammering again, time-trialing toward paradise, which tonight is the Villagio Inn and Spa, honestly the plushest, sweetest hotel I've ever visited: rooms four times bigger than apartments I've lived in; rows of fountains; heated pool; giant hot tub; full-service spa; all-you-can-eat champagne breakfast.

Me, I skip the champagne part in the morning, but I don't hold back on the pastries and lox and fresh fruit, and my life, I all of a sudden realize, has become the happiest blur I can ever remember. Ride all day. Relax all night. Take a sauna, a swim, a hot tub. Have a massage. Have someone read my chakras and tell me, "You're an incredibly complex and awesome person with a substantially mellow aura." Eat as much as humanly possible. Do it again tomorrow.

I'm finding the best climbs in the area, magnificent switchback ascents with spectacular views way up there on the mountaintops, on roads lined with madrone and California live oak and redwoods and giant ferns, with jackrabbits darting among the shrubs and mule deer bounding in the meadows and eagles and vultures circling in the air and, near the ocean, seals barking and waves beating themselves senseless against the rocks.

Somewhere in there, I've ridden away from the ocean and beyond the mountains and into the high desert, and I'm cruising down Butts Valley Road, which I'm still young enough to think is hilarious. I take a break to water the weeds on Butts Valley Road, ha!, and to consult my map. Not far up the road from here, the map tells me, I will reach the point I've been waiting for my entire cycling life. The map's notation reads, "Ink Grade and the southern part of Howell Mountain are two of the area's fabled cycling roads."

Fabled, you say?

Each road gains 1,200 feet in elevation. Cool. Dude, there's no way I'm missing out on one of those. Just happens I reach Ink Grade first—4.4 miles, 1,200 feet up. I can see the road snaking its way westward and upward and vanishing, as great cycling roads always do, into the trees, and I don't hesitate to begin climbing.

I'm used to not drinking now. I'm used to riding a bike instead. I feel like I've been dancing on bikes up mountain roads for years, accelerating through the switchbacks, settling down and powering through the sections when the grade's not so steep, keeping my cadence high, my posture steady and running higher and higher into madrone trees and California live oak and past mule deer and jackrabbits bounding between thickets.

Finally I reach the top and pump a happy fist in the air—a great mountain-stage victory in the fantasy race that my cycling life is—and I stop at Howell Mountain Road.

I should turn west here and descend the mountain and spin easy on through the flat few miles back to Villagio and its excellent hot tub and all my cool buddies on the Back-roads trip, who are no doubt relaxing in Yountville right now. Or I could go east, plummet 1,200 feet in 2.6 miles, turn around, and ride back up.

I plummet. I stop at the bottom, in front of a small auto-body shop, where the men smoking cigarettes on the back porch see me stopping and turning around to climb back from whence I came, and they shake their heads.

I hear one of the men say, "That guy's crazy."

I certainly am.

This hill is steeper, harder, more brutal and soul-shattering in every respect, but I don't care.

I'm cured long before I get to the top.

# 15

No English major in the world hears the word *April* and doesn't think "is the cruelest month." That's just one of those things about April in an English Department. It's the last full month of the university year, when the students have the most homework, the faculty have therefore the most paperwork piling up, and the graduate students defend their theses and dissertations, and the senior undergrads turn their terrified eyes toward the future. It's a tense month for a lot of people, a month leading up inevitably to goodbyes in early May, which is what we do best at the university, say goodbye. We are continually saying goodbye. We prepare people to move on, we tell them they *must* move on, and by God that's what they do.

It hurts to say goodbye, of course, and over the years, in Creative Writing, we have developed a system to ease the pain, as it were, for everyone involved, which is to say when April comes the end-of-year/end-of-education party season begins, and the undergraduates and graduates and faculty alike commence their drawn-out drunken drive toward matriculation. Two, three, four, five days a week, there's something going on, somebody defending a thesis, somebody taking and passing their comprehensive exams, the last workshop, the last day of the second week of partying, could be anything, and it's like let's all go to the bar afterward and have a bunch of drinks and support this person and celebrate this person's accomplishments!

The culmination of the month hereabouts is our MFA Gala Reading, where the poets and the fiction writers who are receiving their masters of fine arts degrees dress up in nice clothes and present themselves, happily and proudly, before the eager literary universe of Southern Illinois University. At the Gala, each of the ten or the twelve graduating students gives a twenty-minute reading of their work, plus, to promote the community spirit of the thing, each graduating student selects someone to write an introduction for them and read *it* aloud, which can run anywhere from three to ten minutes. The entire event lasts a few hours, almost *four,* and if you're not familiar with public readings by authors, if you've never attended one before, let me assure you, a four-hour reading by even an assembly of the greatest living writers in the world seems torturously long.

A big crowd always shows up, though, and ya gotta keep 'em happy, so to keep things lubricated, champagne is served, cases and cases of it, and beer, too, and somehow, during the long reading, despite the crowd's heroic attempts to drink all the booze the department has purchased for the Gala, there's plenty of booze left when the reading's over, and, according to tradition, everybody piles out of the room at school where the reading's been taking place, and we go to a graduate student's house with all the booze and drink till we're blue in the face and till the hour becomes wee and a good number of folks are drunk enough to wee in their pants.

I stand before the world today, April Fool's Day, 2003, thirty-nine years old, a tenured English professor whose job it is to function within this system, and I'll tell you what, looking at this month of April coming up, I'm a lot more stoked about the warm spring weather than about anything having to do with school. I haven't lost interest in being an English professor. I've lost interest in the scene *associated* with being an English professor. I'll grade my papers, teach my classes, sit there with my door open during my office hours, and do all that happy horse manure, but beyond that, I'm completely dead to the April scene at the university. I know it's coming, I know that in the previous three Aprils I've been at the front of the party pack, leading the illimitable charge, buying the shots at the bar or the cases of beer for the after-bar party, but till today or till I went out to California maybe, I haven't recognized the extent of the change I've effected on myself, how dead the old me has become, how much I have become another person with different values and different goals and different ideas about what life means.

I don't know people at school anymore, don't hang around with them ever, don't talk with them unless my job duties require it. In fact, when I see people at school, I often don't recognize them at all; they are forms I once knew, they are puddles I once could see and could enjoy splashing around in, but now they've dried up, and only the ground on which they once formed remains. They are fine people, they just aren't my people anymore.

When I interviewed for my job here, I told these people, I *promised* them, my chief off-duty interest was sitting around at the bar and smoking cigarettes and drinking and engaging in what Socrates instructs us to do with our lives, dialogue. I said, That's *it*. I like to hang out and *talk*. I promised I would be accessible to my students. I promised I would be *there*—whatever *there* means—and available and open to everybody who needed me.

This is what *there* is like: This kid's leaving, that kid's leaving, this class has concluded, this year's in the record books, let's go to the bar and say goodbye. Every April, three, four, five days a week, for the rest of my life. The faces will change, there will be excellent and wonderful and unique students every year who it will break my heart to see go away, but the party will always be the same.

It's not the university's fault, it's not the fault of Creative Writing's *scene*, for sure, that I'm not able to attend one of these gatherings and have a single glass of wine or one can of beer, exchange a few pleasantries, and head home after a moderately short stay. That's *my* fault. *I've* got the alcohol problem, I can't have just one beer. The university doesn't have an alcohol problem, but it's an alcohol-rich environment nevertheless. Even if I *could* find the courage and the wherewithal to hang out at the bar after a thesis defense and not drink a drop, there I'd be at the bar, talking with a bunch of drunk people. It's inconceivable to attend a nighttime Creative Writing social gathering without there being lots of drunk people milling about. I'm talking *drunk* drunk, too—slurring, wobbling, spilling beer. Embarrassing drunk.

Anybody who quits drinking will tell you this: *You must be drunk to find drunk people amusing.*

In April, at midday, in the school hallway, you can smell booze on the graduate students; they're sweating out their hangovers. But they're not losing momentum. Listen to them, they're saying, *You going out tonight? So-and-so's defending her thesis at three.*

"April is the cruelest month." That's the first line of a

T. S. Eliot poem, in case you didn't know, called "The Waste Land." I find the title, the line, the lifestyle, all of it, most ironic.

Look at me on the cover of this book. You think I want to be that guy again? You want me to be that guy again?

I have said goodbye already.

This feels like a confession to say, but it's something I need to accept: My hard days are very hard.

Saturdays and Wednesdays. Those are the days I try to destroy myself, to leave as much of myself on the road as I can. I once saw a homemade videotape of a man pulling his own teeth. He says, before getting to it, "Ashes to ashes, dirt to dirt, you're full of shit if you think this don't hurt." That's my Saturdays and Wednesdays.

But don't feel sorry for me, it's my choice to do this.

The other four days, I ride recovery. A recovery ride is the temporary, short-term equivalent of Long Slow Distance, or LSD, which I'm sorry to say I still think is funny. LSD is the type of riding cyclists commonly do in the winter. The idea behind LSD is to train at a low to moderate intensity for weeks on end in order to build base mileage and to help with endurance. LSD, you might say, is a steady plateau in a cyclist's training, the place from which we vault forward in the spring.

Recovery rides, on the other hand, are rungs in a rising ladder of efforts pointing to peak form somewhere in a season. Recovery gives you a place to pause, to bear your weight and catch your breath before elevating to the next, more difficult event.

Not surprisingly, you ride recovery the same way you ride LSD, easy spinning, could be for three or four hours, at a moderate to low heart rate, the idea being that if your body is trashed from a particularly grueling effort—a hard race, a hard century, or a hard set of intervals on a training ride—you don't stay *off* the bike and sit in a chair till you're rejuvenated, you stay *on* the bike and rejuvenate your trashed body by continuing to move, only at a milder level of exertion.

That's the most important rule of recovery: *You've got to keep moving*.

So if you see me when I'm on the road riding recovery, you'll see a person spinning at a high cadence and going very, very slow, so slow you might assume I suck at cycling and have spent too much money on the race bike I'm riding. But I have to ride that way. That's the routine. Hammer hard, allow the body to recover, *then* hammer even harder.

Sounds an awful lot like drinking to me.

Recovery is part of the regular weekly routine every intelligently trained competitive cyclist goes through—hard, easy, hard, easy—and every intelligent cyclist I know *loves* riding recovery. Why wouldn't they? It's so joyfully easy, so mellow, it's how we know cycling is not only suffering and misery but actually a wonderful pastime, which is what you need to believe cycling is, if you're going to compete on even the most meager level.

*You've got to be having fun, or you won't get anywhere.*

On recovery rides we talk and joke and enjoy the scenery and rehash what happened on Wednesday's hard group ride or on the big race over the weekend and we're laughing most of the time out there, talking loud. On a country road, I'll bet you can hear us coming from a couple of hundred yards away. We probably sound like drunks.

My effort-recovery ladder points toward peaking seven weeks from now at the Assault on Mount Mitchell, on Saturday May 17. That's 103 miles and 11,000 feet of climbing, going from Spartanburg, South Carolina, to the highest point in America east of the Mississippi, the summit of Mount Mitchell, 6,680 feet. Before the Bridge to Bridge last fall, I read a sizable stack of material on challenge centuries and climbing mountains on bikes and all that, and everywhere I looked, everybody I talked to, folks agreed that the Bridge to Bridge is hard, but the Assault on Mount Mitchell, it's off the charts, it's the granddaddy of all challenge centuries, it'll break you in half. Obviously, come on now, what else am I going to do ten days after I turn forty but ride in the Assault on Mount Mitchell?

Seems foreordained somehow.

# HEFT ON WHEELS

I'm getting to be a more experienced cyclist, too, which means I'm getting smarter and more calculating, working now from the understanding that you can't get through the big event on passion alone, that there's preparation involved, and with the proper preparation and the proper attitude, a person can do more than merely survive something like the Assault on Mount Mitchell but in fact *excel* at it. That's my goal, of course, I want to *excel*. I want to finish with strength to spare! And to do that, I've got to organize every aspect of my life and point it toward May 17.

This leaves me only six more weekends to prepare, but I've got the schedule, the proper rising ladder of efforts coming up.

First thing, I've got a road race on April 12, the Hillsboro–Roubaix, a hard forty-four miles.

Next couple of weekends, I'm doing hard hilly centuries around Carbondale with Ed.

On May 3, I've got the 3 State 3 Mountain in Chattanooga. One hundred miles, 7,500 feet of climbing.

I turn forty on May 7, which is on a Wednesday, a scheduled massive-effort day, and if you think I'm not planning on going extra hard on the day I turn forty, on my one-year anniversary of not smoking, well, like the Judas Priest song says, you've got another thing coming.

I've another road race on May 10, the fifty-five-mile Highland Rim Cycling Classic in McMinnville, Tennessee.

Then there we are, May 17, the moment of truth,

6:30 a.m., at the start line of the Assault on Mount Mitchell. Me, 750 other cyclists, and the mountain, or however the song should go.

I can imagine somebody from school, one of my colleagues or grad students, hearing me outline my cycling plan and what motivates me, particularly the part when I say I've got to organize *everything* in my life and point it toward riding in the Assault on Mount Mitchell. "See?" the person from school might say. "Cycling's all he cares about."

Sure. It is. Or at least that's what I say to people at school. Why not?

I say, What *should* I care about? Standing around and watching you get *drunk?*

I work here at the university, but I am learning here, too.

In order for learning to occur, a person needs to reach this understanding: *Who you have been is not who you have to be. You are free to change your thinking.*

Saturday, April 12, 2003, is a sunny, sixty-eight-degree, perfectly calm day for the second annual Hillsboro–Roubaix here in Hillsboro, Illinois, a tiny brick-streeted town northeast of St. Louis. I'm lined up for the start, wearing my Team MACK racing uniform, red and white and pale blue. My legs are shaved, used Nair, actually, just last night I did it. My haircut's a buzz under the helmet, and my bicycle's unsurpassed by any bike here, my Litespeed Tuscany, Dura-Ace, Mavic Ksyrium SSL wheels. I spent an hour last night polishing it and lubing it, and it's gleaming, people. It's a noble steed, and anybody here who knows anything about bikes, which is like *everybody* here, knows that my bike is an extremely high-end piece of machinery.

In brief, I look like a *poseur*. An old guy with a five-thousand-dollar bike and access to a bottle of Nair.

Oh well. But if you want to buy a high-end bike and get into road racing, this is something you're going to have to get over, you're gonna look like a poseur, but that's not something to be ashamed of. You can't stop participating in a sport because there are professional-level people who can obliterate you at it. A sport is about a lifestyle, about health and fitness and happiness, and you want to try hard, of course, you want to do your best, but you'll have to accept that other people's best will frequently be better than yours.

That's true of anything, right? There's always going to be somebody who's better than you.

God comes to mind.

My group, Men's Category V, or the beginner's category, is the last group to head out on the course, which is a twenty-two-mile loop that winds into the countryside, over some horrible chip-and-seal roads of the type I'm used to in Carbondale, then back into Hillsboro, up a steep hill and over a mile or so of potholed brick streets, hence the designation *Roubaix*. In France today is the running of the famous Paris–Roubaix, legendary for its cobbles and horrible road conditions, so here we are, same day as the *real* Paris–Roubaix, carrying on with our Illinois version of it.

We Cat V's are a fairly large group, seventy people at the starting line, which is in front of a modern white church that looks as new to the Lord as I am to racing. The Cat V's have been here quite a while, fidgeting, guys moving in and out of line to roll behind a Dumpster in the parking lot and respond to calls of nature, everybody like, all right already, let's get this sucker rolling.

The other races that will be running simultaneously with ours are, as Phil Liggett would say, well down the *parcours* already. The Men's Cat I-II-III, that's the big dogs, with legitimate talent, they started a half an hour ago. Men's Masters thirty-five and up, which Darren is in, started five minutes after that. The women's Cat I-II-III, five minutes after the Masters Men and so on by five minutes through the men's Cat IV and the women's Cat IV and then us, the absolute bottom end of competitive cycling in the lower Midwest, the Men's Cat V's.

We'll do two laps, or forty-four miles, which isn't as long as Darren's race, which will do three laps, or the Men's Cat I-II-III race, which will do four. Two laps, though, forty-four miles, that's still a long ways to go hard, a lot could happen in forty-four miles, and I should be terrified or freaked out or with pre-race butterflies, but I'm not. I'm mellow, I've got low standards and a realistic mindset, I'm doing this race for the experience and as Mount Mitchell preparation, and I'm expecting to get dropped, early and hard, and never catch up. Besides, you stand at a starting line for thirty-five minutes, you're bound to lose some butterflies.

So after we're under way and get a few miles of racing into our legs, when I find that I'm right at the front of the pack and don't feel one bit taxed, this is easy, I'm not pushing at all, wow, and when I cover the breakaway on the climb at the end of the first lap and ramrod through the brick-paved center of town and end up in front again, driving the lead group of fifteen going into the second lap, I can't tell you how surprised I am, how thrilled I am with my performance. The sun, the high speed, the low effort, it's so incredibly fun, I'm thinking. This is a race, sure, but it feels to me no different from group ride, just on different roads and with a different group of people, who, even though I guess I'm trying to beat them, are my friends even though I've never met them till now. These people live like I live, they train hard to ride the bicycles hard; if they lived in Carbondale, I'd be riding with them four or five days a week.

Such magnificent sun, such a nice day, I'm saying that to the other riders around me, talking to them, like it sure is nice to meet you, and isn't cycling fun? They're all thrilled to have made the break, too, because they're all talking the same way as me, like I'm so glad I took up racing, and we sure couldn't ask for a better day for bike ride.

Somewhere in there, a change comes over the race, and it's not friendly anymore. On the last hill into town, when there's six of us left, and then two of us left, cresting the hill together, this punk kid in an orange jersey and me, and we're dropping down at forty-five miles per hour toward a ninety-degree turn, past several deep potholes, and onto the bricks for five hundred yards, and my bike rattles over the bricks and people are in the front yards along the street yelling and hollering go, go, go, and I'm shaking and in the lead and focusing everything, my eyes, my life, forward down the bricks, and I'm thinking I'm going to win the bike race and everything I hate about myself is gone, everything I'm embarrassed about is gone, every time I've drunk too much or eaten too much or not cared enough, all of it, the harder and harder I push down the bricks, gone, gone, gone, then bam, a hard ninety-degree left and the last two hundred straightaway toward the finish and, like in the e.e. cummings poem, one-two-three-four-five guys blow past me, and it's too late. I sit up in the saddle and finish sixth.

What's happened, I guess, is I ended up leading those five riders over the bricks, allowed them to draft off of me, and when I was blown and coasting around that last corner, they blew me away. Not by a long distance, really—five or ten yards, tops, at the line—but I still lost.

A couple of days later, when I'm at school and wearing my Hillsboro–Roubaix T-shirt and telling students what happened, they're like, Oh, interesting, or when I'm trying to explain it to my colleagues, they're like, Is that so? I remember the race, I say, in blurs and flashes, how totally hard it was at the end, banging and rattling over the bricks, a slow-motion film I see of people clapping alongside the road and children hollering go, go, go, *allez, allez, allez, vite, vite, allons-y,* and how my memory is in a tunnel-vision view, maybe the experience itself was in a tunnel-vision view. But that's the thing, it really happened, I was really in the *lead* at the end of my first road race, and surely, in hindsight, I could have won it. Real. It was *real*. Much of what we do, I say to people at school, is theoretical, and here's something actual and true. Not a metaphor I lived through. A *real* bike race.

*What do you expect me to do,* a sour graduate student tells me one day, *start riding a bike?*

I say, metaphorically, *Yes.*

On recovery ride, on Sunday and Monday and Tuesday, I tell Gerald or Darren or Don or anybody with me that I feel like I'm floating again, that I'm focused in on the events ahead, and despite the fact that I blew it, tactically, at the end of my first race, dammit, I was right there in contention at the end, which means I don't care if Cat V is the lowest of the low, I still have become a very strong cyclist. I'm not faking it. The bicycle has become an extension of my body.

Wednesday, on group ride, I prove it. I'm one of the

local big dogs now. Doesn't matter who shows up anymore, I never get dropped, I'm always at the front, I'm really the real deal.

When I dream at night, I feel my legs spinning in circles.

My wife says in my sleep I speak in French:

*Allez, allez, allez.*

*Vite, vite.*

*Allons-y.*

The Gala is on a Friday night, in a cut-off section of cafeteria in the Student Center, near a glass door that opens to an outside patio, where it's nice for the smokers, seventy out of the one hundred in attendance, to take their drinks and burn a few cigarettes and shoot the breeze they're befouling before the reading begins and during the thirty-minute intermission and even after the reading, people outside smoking and belting down champagne.

It's a wonderful reading, everybody says. The graduates look so nice in their dress-up clothes. We're so proud of them.

Later, at the traditional get-drunk-at-the-grad-student's-house party, I'm walking around drinking a Diet Pepsi, out of the can; it's either that or booze, basically, which will show you what's available for the nondrinker types at a party. Not that I'm saying I deserve special treatment. Quit drinking, that doesn't mean you're *special*. Just means you might feel exceptionally sober when you're at a party

But hey, I will try to be a better person. I will enjoy myself with my Diet Pepsi. I really love Diet Pepsi and standing around listening to drunk people saying the same thing over and over.

For instance, here's a student I'm talking to, an undergrad but no kid, a guy in his thirties named Keith. Keith's big and strong and says he used to be a boxer and now works part-time at a landscape company digging up trees with his bare hands or whatever. A year ago I was considerably larger than him, outweighing him by probably thirty pounds. I've had him in a few classes and have spoken dismissively of his literary talents, remarks he hasn't appreciated, and now he outweighs me by forty pounds. He keeps coming up to me, wobbly and loud, putting his gorilla-like arm around my shoulder and saying, "Little man, I should kick your ass."

Does it five or ten times, and people laugh every time.

Another guy, a fellow considerably younger and smaller, a grad student, he's outside with the smokers and every fifteen minutes or so pops inside to use the bathroom or to get another beer, and I like the guy and believe he's got much potential. I even recruited him to come here and study with me. I say to him, "Did you enjoy the reading?"

He says, "I blabba yamma blabba yamma."

My sentiments exactly.

Another student, female grad student, says to me, "There he is, Mr. Diet Pepsi."

Twenty-one years ago, in late April, I lived in Towers Hall at the University of Wisconsin–Eau Claire. I had long hair and a beard and wore torn bib overalls and torn T-shirts and was in general cultivating the reprobate-lumber-jack-intellectual look. I really wasn't a reprobate, I was a music major who would sit in a practice room most every afternoon playing the piano, and every evening, after supper, I was into partying and telling people I had spent the afternoon playing the piano.

That's cool, isn't it? That's not hurting anything.

Late one afternoon in April then, I had walked back to my dorm from playing the piano and was coming in the lobby, four-thirty on a Friday, whistling and happily shuffling my feet. I stopped to pick up my mail and then made my way toward the elevator, which I would then take up to my room on the fifth floor. Some kids I didn't recognize, clean-cut farm-kid types, were in the lobby, and one among them, a muscular square-jawed guy, took a look at me and announced to everyone, "There he is, Mr. Doper."

I've been angry about that for twenty-one years, not because I didn't look the part of Mr. Doper and in fact *act* the part of Mr. Doper, but because of the rudeness involved. There I am in the Towers Hall lobby, happy after practicing my piano and minding my own business, and wham, it's that kid's failure to recognize how much more goes on in a human being than a simple categorical label can summarize.

Mr. Diet Pepsi.

The next morning, Ed comes over to my place at six-thirty to ride a hundred miles over a course I've been designing lately, my attempt to come up with the hilliest possible hundred-mile loop in southern Illinois, and this ride is certifiably difficult, I guarantee it. Come and ride it with me sometime, you'll freak how hard it is.

Ed's going to ride in the 3 State 3 Mountain with me next weekend in Chattanooga, and the idea today is we're going to blast through a hard hundred miles at event pace, meaning we can stop a couple of times, briefly, to pee and to fill water bottles, but otherwise we're pushing it all day. Get through this, recover nicely during the week, do a few surges on Wednesday, take a day off, easy ride on Friday, then next Saturday, when we're riding up real mountains in a real mountain range, we'll be able to hang with the top group.

We are men of science, I say to Ed, and he thinks that's pretty funny.

We're a couple of nuts riding bikes.

This is how perfect things are, no wind, cloudy but dry, seventy degrees. We cut loose, we jam up every climb, we work together in the flats, sharing the draft, we eat PowerBars and drink a bottle of Gatorade every hour, we stay focused on pressing the attack forward. A couple of times in there I drop Ed, really drop Ed hard, near the top of the longest climbs, and it occurs to me, during these moments, that I should ride back to Ed and turn around and drop him again up the hill before he can crest it the first time, like he had done to me two years ago. I should rub it totally in his face and be a dick about it, but I get to the top, ahead of Ed, and slow down till he catches my wheel again. Ed doesn't say anything about it, I don't say anything about it.

We're both riding really hard, is what matters, working together, not winning or losing or proving we're superior to each other.

Saki says, *Ride together.*

I know what that's about now: If you attack and drop somebody on the road, you are a creating a situation where you will ride alone, and if you drop somebody repeatedly during the course of a ride, you effectively are informing the person with whom you have agreed to ride for *six hours* that, *Hey, I'm better than you, man. See how I keep dropping you? Why should I be riding with you in the first place, if you can't keep up?* You may be stronger, but you are alone off the front and proving something hollow and empty and never true: *I am superior to you.*

So if I say that because I don't drink anymore, I have advanced beyond the level of the heavy drinkers at the university, I am wrong indeed. I'm no better than them, they're no better than me. What we're doing, in fact, is remarkably similar. We are engaged in a pastime, a recreation, a *community* activity.

No one wants to drink alone, right? By extension, the people who can drink the most, the people who are the best at drinking, they don't shy away from more-moderate drinkers, do they? Hell no. It's more fun in numbers!

Maybe the logic isn't the same in cycling, but it's close. Ride *together* for six hours with someone, or with several people, enjoy the conversation and the camaraderie, it's more fun, it's a more enriching experience all around.

With this in mind, after I've ridden ninety-five miles or so with Ed and we're cruising side by side back into Carbondale, I ask Ed if he's had a good ride.

He says, "You betcha."

I knew that's what he'd say.

# 16

Not because it's there.

Or because I haven't smoked a cigarette for exactly one year and two
weeks or because, for ten months now, I
haven't had a drop of beer or wine or
bourbon or because I'm stupid enough to believe, if I can
ride my bicycle up the biggest mountain road in North
America east of the Mississippi, if I can finish the Assault
on Mount Mitchell with a respectable result, a respectable
elapsed time, I'm going to obtain redemption for all the
horrible things I've done and said drunk. But I really
believe that. I want redemption.

Not because on the History Channel two weeks ago _____

in my hotel room in Chattanooga, Tennessee, I heard the opening strains of the Soviet national anthem, and since that moment, no matter how many times I've tried these last fourteen days, in Chattanooga and, seven days later, in McMinnville, Tennessee, and today in the Carolinas, I've not been able to shut the Soviet national anthem off. It's with me, the music of epic proletarian struggle, and I very much would like to be done with struggle now. I've proven, beyond any reasonable objection, my ability to join the struggle and to labor in pursuit of the I-don't-know-what that middle-aged sport is.

Not because I crashed at the fifteenth mile, either, coming into a ninety-degree corner and a narrow bridge in a pack of 250 cyclists going thirty miles per hour, and bikes are going down everywhere, and whammo, I'm on the ground, slammed into my left hip, and struggling to get up and to remount my bike and go on, and you want to know the root cause of this misery? Rain. This is the problem: rain. Driving rain for the Assault on Mount Mitchell, and that's why I crashed, because exactly like in the Bridge to Bridge, I'm in a deluge, only this time there's no adventure involved, no nobility or achievement of any of that horsepucky. I've ridden up mountain roads in the rain before. It sucks, that's all there is to it.

And not because I'm a dry drunk. That's a good reason for it to be raining today. I'm a dry drunk who's got it coming to him. You've been following my story so far; you're an expert on me. You think it's possible I've trained all this time to ride in the Assault on Mount Mitchell because I'm a dry drunk? Because if I'm finally honest, if I cut through all this exercise crap, I'll have to admit that what I really want more than anything in the world is to get drunk? Could that be it?

Look at the evidence: angry at work and irritable and maniacally obsessed with exercise, overjoyed sometimes, withdrawn others. Or what about my behavior on New Year's or at the Gala? Just a bit on the edgy-slash-cranky side? It's dry-drunk behavior, people. Classic. I've heard this behavior often takes years to pass, because it's such a monumental undertaking, if you're a drunk, to say, *Okay, never again*.

Or it's not monumental to say, *Okay, never again*; it's monumental to maintain it forever.

No.

It's because we all need somewhere to get to. It's because you can't get anywhere without a destination. It's because there's no point in having a small, innocuous destination. You get there too quickly, been there, done that, and what do you do then? My life has needed a Mount Mitchell looming before me and terrifying me, but now that I'm here and on the mountain, I'm not sure I remember why.

For the four months leading up to this day, I've let *everything* in my life slide except for the things I needed to do to train for this event, and now it's raining and cold and I've crashed hard and all that training and sacrifice, it wasn't worth it. What would be worth it, however, is a beer, you betcha, a large ice-cold tallboy beer, right now, in North Carolina, on the Blue Ridge Parkway, in the fog and rain, because this is not cycling weather but sit-in-the-tavern-and-play-dice weather.

But here's the situation, ain't no beer to be had. I'm on my bicycle, seventeen miles away from the finish of the Assault on Mount Mitchell, and I can say with confidence that my legs are shot, my confidence is shot, I'm barely able to turn over the pedals, and I never want to ride a bicycle again.

This rain is not driving, merely steady, a rain emerging from the very cloud I'm riding through, and I figure I'm running in about one-hundredth place right now, but I don't really know. There's nothing to see anywhere—a cyclist in an orange vest maybe, way up the road, thirty yards maybe, the limit of my eyesight in the fog. I occasionally hear someone coughing behind me.

The Soviet national anthem plays again. Pretty soon I'll be hearing a big military truck with an ICBM on it pulling past me, why not? I sure as hell ain't gonna *see* it.

What I like about drinking is it's easy. Sit there. Order beer. Smoke cigarette. Order more beer. After an hour, do a couple of shots. Get hungry: get some peanuts or whatever. Laugh. Whatever. It hurts later, the next day or maybe even the next two or three days, but the hurt can always be made to go away. Can we say blender drinks?

I can look at this two ways. (1) I have seventeen miles to go. Or (2) I have come eighty-six miles so far.

# HEFT ON WHEELS

So far, starting several hours ago, I left with the pack of 750 cyclists, in a pouring-down rain and in the dark, from Spartanburg, South Carolina, and I crashed on my hip at mile fifteen and got back on my bike, and I guess that's noble and proof I'm tough. Like look how hard I've been pounding ever since, through the seventy-three-mile mark at Marion, North Carolina, where my wife and daughters were waiting for me in the rain, having a miserable time, to give me a fresh bottle of Gatorade when I passed by. They've taken a school bus to the top of the mountain, and I'm sure they're wet and having a rotten time at the top right now.

Between Marion and the top, incidentally, in thirty miles, there's roughly 6,500 feet of elevation gain, half of which I've climbed already. I'm rain-soaked totally, all the way into my spirit, my hip's killing me, there's nothing to see up the road but grayness and an empty unsatisfying void. I am completely alone in space and time, and I've never driven on this road, never seen this road, the Blue Ridge Parkway leading to the entrance to Mount Mitchell State Park, but I've read lots about it, it goes up, and it's not going to quit going up till it reaches the highest point in America east of the Mississippi.

God comes to me. I've never seen Him before, and I can't see Him now. I just know He's there somewhere in the thick fog.

"What's your problem?" He says.

"The Soviet national anthem," I say, "it won't stop playing."

He says, "Tell me the truth now."

I say, "I've taken this biking thing way too far. I never meant to hurt myself like this. I want to be the guy I used to be again."

God says, "Be quiet for a while, listen to the rain hitting the road."

It hisses like a snake, which I guess is how God means for rain to sound when it hits a road, because that's sort of what He says. "That's not the sound of pain, that's the sound of your spirit breaking."

I pull up on another cyclist and grind past him, he's in his rhythm, I'm in mine, both of us are hurting, and I say to the guy, "Man, this is torture."

The guy says, "Savor it. This is as good as it gets."

I get past him and can hear him breathing behind me for a few minutes till finally the sound of him fades away, and God's back with me.

God says, "That guy back there, his spirit's not broken."

"Leave me alone for a while," I say.

"You are alone," He says. "That's what I'm trying to tell you."

Speaking of Russia, the underground man in Dostoyevsky's *Notes from the Underground* is forty years old. That, among other things, causes him tremendous consternation, and he says, "Living past forty is indecent, vulgar, immoral! Now answer me, sincerely, honestly, who lives past forty? I'll tell you who does: fools and scoundrels."

The underground man needs to get out and ride a bike and find something else to complain about.

Ten days ago, when I turned forty, it didn't mean anything, it didn't feel like anything, I didn't feel smarter or dumber or like I was doing anything special. Now, when I turned thirty-nine, dude, *that* was momentous, *that* was giving up smoking and accepting middle age and getting the courage together to commit my energies to living a healthier life; now all the changes have been made, and I have become habituated to the lifestyle. I've done everything right. I've turned forty and been in the best shape of my life when I turned. That's great. But what do I do now? Pedal up a mountain in the rain, because it's there?

I won't remember much of the rest of the ride, it's too traumatic, too hard. All that training, all that dedication, and what have I done? Still managed to underestimate the mountain.

I'll remember the last part of Mount Mitchell, the last twenty yards, which is how far away from the finish line I am before I can even see it. I see the world coming into a hazy focus and the time clock showing my elapsed time, six hours and twelve minutes, a good result, I guess, and I see my wife and my two little girls soaking wet and standing there waiting for me, and I roll my bike to a stop. A forest ranger, a big guy who can see I'm in distress, hands me my official Assault on Mount Mitchell finisher's patch and pats me on the shoulder. I try getting off my bike and can't. Ends up, my wife and two course workers have to hold me up and pry the bike away from me. I hug my wife and tell her, "I'm going to be a better person, I'll really try to be a better person."

I don't know if this is a moment of triumph or of pathetic desperation.

The Soviet national anthem has stopped playing in my head, and I don't have strength left in me to cry.

# 17

$A$fter Mount Mitchell, I become aimless.

I should take time off the bike. I'm not enjoying the bike like I used to, it's work, it's drudgery, it's a ball and chain, it's not getting me anywhere but into more hurt. The medical truth here, I know this from reading up on it, is I'm feeling the symptoms of severe overtraining, manifesting itself in depression and thirst and tiredness. Feels like a hangover, which is your built-in irony. Take the cumulative effects of beating the crap out of my body for too many months in a row, doing this in the name of health, and how do I feel? Like I've got a _____ hangover. I know the cure, too. I should step away from cycling for a week, or maybe even two weeks, use the extra free time to take the kids to the beach, go to the zoo, that kind of thing, but I'm too fried to be thinking straight.

Something went wrong during Mount Mitchell. Cycling changed from a torture I was using for positive personal gain into a torture that was just plain old grubass horrible torture. It sucked. I am angry that this has occurred. Something as important to me as cycling, to risk burning out on it and never riding again! Terrible. No excuse for it.

First thing I'm going to blame, I'm too fat.

Look at a great cyclist, then look at me, don't matter how much leaner I am than I used to be, I'm still carrying too much extra, and it's hurting me in the mountains, dude. It *is*. If I could get my body-fat percentage down to four percent—I'm serious—which would mean losing fifteen or twenty pounds and dropping below 160 pounds, now that would change things a lot right there, don't you think?

This pisses me off, actually. I had it licked, I was well on my way to reducing to 160 in February, it was merely a matter of sticking with it a little longer, but I wasn't able to butch out the stomach pain and maintain the strict diet. I slacked off and took it easy and opted for comfort and quality of life over performance on the road. I ate too much, I enjoyed the fueling process too much, I was overly amazed by the happy balance you can achieve when you

# HEFT ON WHEELS

take in five thousand calories and turn around and *expend* five thousand calories. So sure, I've been feeling good since I've been eating the proper quantities. Till Mount Mitchell, I've been having a pleasant go of things, but the fact remains, I've been roughly 175 pounds since the first of the year.

That's fifteen pounds more than I need.

I paid for that extra weight, no doubt about it, on the Blue Ridge Parkway rising to Mount Mitchell State Park.

So I'm thinking for the time being, since I don't have any events planned, nothing, not till maybe the second week of July, when there's a road race near here that Darren's been saying we should do, and after that, not till September and the Bridge to Bridge, but that's so far away I can't even imagine it. I've been thinking since, at 175 pounds, I can eat as much as I want and maintain that weight, that were I to drop, right now, in the next month or so, down to 160 pounds, then I would be able to eat as much as I want at that weight and maintain it, and when I show up for the starting line for the Bridge to Bridge in September, I'll be able to take an *hour* off my time from last year.

That's right, if I want to make a run at dropping those last fifteen pounds that need to go, now's the time.

I get back on the bike on May 19, after a day off to travel back from North Carolina, and I don't take a single day off till, well, almost the end of June.

It doesn't help. I go back to my starvation-sequence diet. But I don't lose any weight. I'm unhappy and irritable. I know I have to keep cycling, that I want to excel at it, but what about the rest of my life? The career I used to keep upfront and center in my mind. My family. My old friends. My mind itself, what about *that*?

I'm riding with Don a week or so after Mount Mitchell, and he's of course supportive of my crazy cycling quests and is asking about what happened during the big ride, and I lay this business on him about me being too fat. He's a small man, no more than 135 pounds, and is as mild-tempered as anybody I've known in my life, a genuinely nice guy, but he's got a major temper, particularly when somebody like me, who is in the kind of physical shape I'm in, says he's too fat. He yells at me for a three-hour ride and then for several three-hour rides after that.

I promise him I think he's right, I'm not fat, but I keep trying to starve myself, though not with as much success as I used to have.

I get hungry these days, I eat. It's hard to starve successfully under such conditions.

I never did go to treatment. I should have probably. That's been a big worry I've had all along through my 180-degree turn in life, that I've been devising my own treatment methods, and because my methods are so improvisational and extreme, they might be doomed from the get-go. They say, for instance, depressed people often drink alcohol or take drugs to self-medicate. By extension, a depressed person can devise a health-and-fitness plan to self-medicate. I mean, it's the same thing, isn't it? Surely health and fitness is a better option than, say, rum and coke, but it fills the same void. It's about preventing sadness, it's about feeling good.

My problem, obviously, is I don't by nature do things in moderation. I have what you might call a gigantic appetite for life and for whatever I'm doing in it. In my drinking days, I was always a hard-charging party animal, in there hammering down the drinks till bar time and beyond, a guy who loved partying and thought people who couldn't drink in the bar for hours on end were weenies; with cycling, I'm basically the same kind of fanatic, completely overtaken by it, it's all I think about, I am maniacally obsessed by it.

I'm an enthusiast, okay?

Always overdoing it, riding 110 miles when I could easily get the same health benefits from fifty-five, but at least I'm *into* it, I'm *passionate* about it.

Am I scaring you? I should be. I'm scaring myself.

But that's a good sign. That's right, being scared is definitely a positive sign, proof that through all this I have become self-aware. Take away the booze, give my brain its full allotment of oxygen, *voilà*, I'm self-aware. Fancy that. My brain is clear to the point of becoming too clear, quite frankly, and the whole whooshing nature of my change has filled me with righteousness and a form of high-on-life arrogance that I can understand full well might annoy people who aren't quite as *into* it as me. I've become the self-righteous health-freak snob I used to hate, is what's happened. But I'm not complaining, and I'm not ashamed. It's not every year a person loses eighty pounds and increases his physical fitness by a kabillion levels. What am I supposed to do? Keep my head down and pretend that nothing's happened?

True, I might have done everything the wrong way, taken too many stupid risks with extreme diet and intense exercise, and I could easily have caused my body tremendous damage in the process, could have had a heart attack or a stroke or bonked myself into diabetic coma out there training hard with no food in my guts or God only knows what else could have beset me. I'll give you some advice, though: *Be more careful than me.* If I had to do it over—no, that's ridiculous. I don't have to do it over.

A couple other things keep nagging at me. Like I'm convinced I'm a horrible father and have been since I made my first major venture back into cycling, when I lived in Eau Claire the summer before moving to Carbondale.

This is a few years ago, when I'm still eighty pounds overweight, when I'm the guy on the cover of this book, and I'm heading out on a May afternoon for a thirty-mile ride. Cloudy skies, a possibility of light rain. I still have my old Miyata 512, a good bike but a bit rusty. I can't afford a fancy bike yet. I'm not a professor yet. I'm a lecturer at the university in Eau Claire, my alma mater, teaching a few sections of English Composition and drinking three days a week and feeling fairly depressed, which is why I'm going biking.

Except this is the middle of the afternoon, and I'm not doing any work to speak of and can only afford for my family to live in a four-plex, in an industrial park, next to some railroad tracks, near the freeway. What else? I've got a four-year-old daughter in day care, I've got a pregnant wife working her fingers to the nub at a nursing home, and here I am, instead of working, I'm hung over and going out for a thirty-mile spin, to sweat some booze from my system.

So I live fairly close to the day care, and I'm not taking the road that leads to the day care because I'm the type of parent who spies on his children, who feels the urge to check up on his children, which is proof of what I'm saying about being a horrible father right there, I don't feel the urge to check up on my children. I'm taking this road past my daughter's day care because it's the only low-traffic road out of town.

I'm pedaling along, a gray day, mid-fifties, headwind, not an ideal day for cycling, and up ahead I see something like a large animal on the road ahead, an enormous white head and a snaking tail. But the closer I get I can see it's a large woman leading a group of small children down the road. Closer yet, that's my daughter's day-care class—the kids holding a rope and singing "Polly Wolly Doodle" in the wrong-note high-pitched way that day-care kids always do, the way that brings a smile to grandmothers' faces at the Spring Sing. A line of children holding a rope.

My Annie's in the middle, happily trudging along, concentrating on the words in the song—she likes to sing, what kid doesn't?—and when I slow to a stop next to the line and say, "Hi, Annie," she looks up for a long while in my direction and doesn't register that it's her daddy in that floppy yellow sweatshirt, that big man on a rusty blue bike.

The teacher does a similar nonrecognition, a combination of (1) who's this guy? (2) what's this guy doing riding a bike in the middle of the day? (3) doesn't he have a job to go to? and (4) why isn't he taking care of his kid if he doesn't have anything better to do than go biking?

Then the teacher says, as if to assure her charges that the big man is not as scary as he looks, "Hi, Annie's dad."

Annie's dad.

And Annie smiles, just for the briefest second, says, "That's my dad," and holds the rope again and waits to start singing again.

The clouds are a deep gray, maybe a spit of rain's in there, a small spit that could come and go without anybody noticing, and the wind carries a chill.

"I'll pick you up later," I say, and Annie doesn't respond, stares over in my direction, and the rope starts moving and she's singing again.

These are the days when my wife's shift starts at seven

in the morning. She works full-time, plus every other weekend, while being pregnant, and when we move later this summer from Eau Claire to Carbondale, she'll quit her job, of course, and move to Carbondale right when the baby's due. We'll have lived in Carbondale for six days, in fact, when our daughter Helen is born.

Can you imagine? Two kids, a new town, a new house, no sleep because of the baby, and the four-year-old being a four-year-old. My poor wife.

There I am through this, getting back on my bicycle and staying on my bicycle, and of course still drinking heavily three-four nights a week and smoking a pack of Marlboro Mediums a day. But the great moving-forward will be occurring, the great unshifting of behavior fault lines will be occurring which, in two years, will give me the necessary inertia I need to make a successful 180-turn in my life.

See what I'm saying? It's come at the expense of other people.

This is wrong, I think, but I don't know what else to do but lay it out there.

This is a serious fault, no doubt. I, I, I. My children: nothing to do with it. My wife: nothing to do with it. My relatives, my born-and-raising: nothing.

For my entire life, my biggest personal obstacle has been the combination of obesity and depression and sloth, and the cure for this has been riding a bicycle. I have cured myself. This does not make me a good person, or a kind person, just a man who's found a way to make himself feel better.

Himself. His Highness. He who will be gone with his middle-aged cycling buddies every Sunday morning from six till noon-thirty or two. He who will be gone evenings five-thirty till eight-thirty every Monday, Wednesday, and Friday during daylight savings time for group ride at the bike shop. He who says, Gee, group ride's not enough. I'll have to go on a ninety-minute *pre*-ride before group ride. Who will be gone on an easy recovery ride to points unknown every Tuesday and Thursday afternoon. Who, if he's not racing on Saturdays, will simply have to go out and simulate race conditions for at least three hours. Five hours, if possible. Who spends two hundred, three hundred, four hundred, five hundred bucks a month on tires, tubes, cables, brakes, brake pads, spokes, bolts, saddles, heart-rate monitors, Gatorade, PowerBars, PowerGels, protein powder, bibshorts, jerseys, socks, gloves, and books on the human need for glycogen. Who falls asleep every night reading these books or the catalogs from World Cycling Productions or Performance Bicycle or Bike Nashbar or Colorado Cyclist or SuperGo or, once a month, *Bicycling* magazine or *Cycle Sport* or *Velo News*.

Him.

Way overboard, no doubt. But being overboard with cycling and clean living has produced a phenomenal change in my attitude. I think it's because cycling and clean living is such an overwhelmingly positive combination, it produces the desire to be good, to strive to improve. For instance, cycling has actually helped me to be a better family man than I ever was—not perfect by any stretch, but better. When I was heavy drinker, I never would have asked my wife, *You think I'm getting drunk too much? Does it piss you off, dear, that I didn't get home from that after-bar party till four-thirty in the morning?* Now that I'm a hardcore cyclist, I do ask my wife if I'm cycling too much. I make a point of it, to open the lines of communication with her, to ask her *Is this bothering you?* She says it's good to see me happy, keep cycling, why would that bother her? Besides, she says, you're always home at night.

I don't know why this occurs to me now, but check it out. What I need to do is become fanatical about living a balanced life, one in which I approach everything with moderation and a relaxed mindset and a mellow set of expectations. I mean, I could be totally *insane* about exercising *restraint*. Wow. I have to ponder that one for a while and get back to you. My first thoughts on the subject— well, let's just say I'll take it under consideration.

Reminds me of an old saw I've been playing for my students for years: *Do as I say, but don't do as I do.*

My goal should be to say, *Do as I do.*

We've got a new guy rides recovery with us on Sundays, name of Tony. He's a philosopher, literally. He's a philosophy professor. Wears a beret and everything, or I've been told he does. I've never seen Tony when he's not in his cycling gear.

That's a common thing for cyclists to say to each other, by the way, when they bump into each other in a noncycling environment: "I didn't recognize you with your clothes on."

Years and years ago, when Tony was, I can only assume, a philosophical teenager, he was a champion bowler in Portland, Oregon. His father owned a bowling alley and, as bowling-alley owners often do, passed along the art of godlike bowling to his son. Tony has bowled fourteen American Bowling Congress–sanctioned 300 games, and five 299 games. Awesome, no? And bowling begat ballet dancing to improve, much like the great bowler Fred Flintstone once did, his musculoskeletal control on the approach to the lane. And from the ballet came a stint with a ballet troupe in New York in his twenties; from New York, as has happened to many before him, came philosophy; and just in case this hasn't been enough, Tony has lived for long periods in Europe and has climbed rock faces and crossed boulder fields in Germany, Switzerland, France, and probably Swaziland for all I know. I tell people that Tony has climbed the Matterhorn, but he hasn't climbed the Matterhorn. The Matterhorn might be just plain too easy a climb for Tony. He's forty-four, happily married and the father of two exceptionally gifted children. He's a good father, too.

What am I saying about him? I think that I've been

striving all this time to become a person like him, healthy, engaged in life, with varied interests, happy.

Maybe, finally, I'm there.

So this is a Sunday morning in late June of 2003, and I've got my good attitude back. It's been six weeks since Mount Mitchell, and the sting of that day has finally begun to recede. Tony and me and a couple of other guys and Don and Gerald meet up at my house, six o'clock sharp, and exchange pleasantries about gear, clothing, and sunglass-tint selection and about the grand heaps of pasta or potatoes we crammed down the night before to give us fuel for the long roll before us.

We start easily enough out of Carbondale, spinning, letting the bike's momentum propel us from the dead college town that Carbondale is, this time of year, this day of the week, this time of morning, to the dead countryside that rural southern Illinois always is between here and the twenty miles over the Shawnee Hills to the Mississippi River. Not a cloud in the sky, the summer heat aches to rise from the asphalt and shimmy across the Shawnee and the cornfielded floodplain near the river, and we descend from the hills, pedaling easy, a flock of geese training for a migration that might never come. When we reach the bottomland, we head south down the flatlands of Illinois Route 3 and form ourselves into a rotating pace line, pulling each other along in thirty-second turns for the next hour, nobody saying a word, a cough here and there, someone announcing a car up or a car back. This is the essence of our sport, the quiet, the wordlessness, the easy whoosh down the road on a Sunday morning; it is the truth, the deliverance from the tavern, from evil, from our lives.

Eventually, about forty-five miles into it, we stop and refill our water bottles at a small picnic area in the Trail of Tears State Park. Nothing much here: just a concrete pavilion, a latrine, a water spigot. And we've been gone for a few hours, and we've got a few more hours out there yet to go, and we're very happy and very healthy, as long as we're out here riding our bikes.

Note that this is not a family experience. This is an individual thing we do *away* from all that. We deal with our families later, after the ride.

But this isn't a bad situation. We're riding bikes. How bad can that be? This is Sunday morning, we'll be back home by noon or at the latest one o'clock, and it's not like we're piling on home drunk in the middle of the night after watching the ballgame at the tavern and hanging out doing shots for three hours afterwards.

When I get back from the ride, I feel great. My daughters are playing in the backyard, running through the sprinkler, and my wife's reading a book under the shade tree. I put my bike away and take a shower and hang with my family for the rest of the day. We pile in the car and drive to a Mexican restaurant for lunch, then we wander around the mall for a while, enjoying, as my wife and I like to say, somebody else's air-conditioning. We have a few laughs, we look at this and that, we buy a few things, we talk about buying some others. Later in the afternoon, when my younger daughter goes down for her nap, I go biking with the older one, Annie, who is six years old and has gone beyond training wheels and wants to get out there and hammer like her daddy does, and to give her her propers, she's really strong, she could be a racer someday, if she wants to. We beat around the university campus for an hour, then come back home, hot and happy, and tell the family what an awesome time we had on our ride. After supper we all go to the playground at the municipal park, and the girls go nuts on the slides and swings and so forth, and my wife and I sit on a bench and shoot the breeze about what fine children we have, how nice things have turned out since we quit smoking, how much happier the family is since I gave up drinking and carrying on. Life's so much better now than it ever was.

By nine o'clock, we're all in bed, the whole Magnuson family, sound asleep.

The next evening, on Monday group ride, I'm the strongest rider. I weigh 173 pounds. And a truck will hit me.

# 18

Get hit by a truck, and live, and you'll think God's given you a second chance on life. You will. You'll think you can start over from scratch.

The morning after the accident, even though only with extreme difficulty am I able to sit up or stand up and walk or do anything—even sprawling on the couch or sitting in a chair and breathing hurts like hell—I take my daughter Annie to her ten-thirty ballet lesson at the Student Recreation Center. She's almost seven now, I can't believe she's almost seven. She's very self-assured and friendly, a good conversationalist, a pleasant person. She's patient with me, too, and how I'm walking slowly through the parking lot. She's announcing to people when we pass them, to clarify any potential misunderstanding, "My dad got hit by a truck."

I sure do look bad: limping, stiff-backed, bandages alongside my right eye and on my knuckles and elbow. I look like somebody dropped me off a building, which isn't all that far from the truth, I flew in spirals twenty-five feet through the air.

I feel strangely relieved, to tell the truth. I've avoided a horrible fate, that was a close call there yesterday evening, and if I've ever been ready for a legitimate, nobody-can-call-you-a-weenie excuse to ease up for a while and take stock, now is it.

I get my daughter settled in to her ballet class and wander around to a large commons area in the rec center with some comfortable leather couches, and I sit, sink in, exhale through the pain in my ribs, and look around. Across the commons area from me, there's the equipment desk, where the students can check out basketballs and jump ropes and weightlifting belts and material associated with the life spent in movement. A couple of guys are working the counter, lean and happy. Summer semester, and business is slow. Other side of the commons, there's the cardio room with its TVs and treadmills and stairsteppers and elliptical trainers and stationary bikes and one Spinning bike. The cardio room's basically vacant at the moment, which I don't imagine is unusual for midmorning in summer. A couple of souls, though, three or four women, one lone pudgy guy with a large tattoo of a dragon on his calf, they're in there working up a sweat and watching TV and going nowhere.

The world has stopped moving.

I get back on my feet, of course. You know *me*. I hobble in to the cardio room and wrench myself up on that Spinning bike, and in my T-shirt and jeans and tennis shoes I pedal slow circles for ten minutes or so. My left leg hurts so bad there's no way I can do even something basic like stand up in the saddle and spin easy, but I can pedal, I can make circles with my feet. I'll be cured in time, I can tell it right now. I simply have to be patient with this.

That afternoon at one, for the first Tuesday afternoon in I can't remember, I'm at home with nothing to do. My wife and kids are off at the beach, I believe—they've learned to go ahead and do whatever they want in the afternoons because I'm always on the bike in the afternoons—so it's not like, now that I happen to be around the house for one afternoon, they're going to change their schedule. So I climb the stairs to my study and sit in my reading chair and do what I know I need to do now: look around, take stock.

The last time I got drunk, nearly a year ago—it was on July fourth—I had some grad students over to burn some meat on the Weber grill and release the malt from several cases of Budweiser. When I was lubed and in high-octane drinking mode late at night, I had people up in my study to crank tunes. I played them CDs and cassettes of music I dig, unusual stuff that grad students in English don't usually listen to. A bunch of instrumental jazz rock stuff, in case you're interested. Anyway, I'd play one song off this CD, one song off that CD, and then put another in and not bother putting the CD or cassette back in its case. Yanked out five or six CDs and ten or twelve cassettes, figured I'd pick up the mess later, and there they are, a year later, and I haven't touched them. They're thick with dust, so much dust I'm afraid I'll ruin the CDs scraping the crud off. Surrounding the base of my computer screen and in the cracks and crannies of my desk and under the desk, there's cigarette ash left from more than a year ago, and look in that corner, a cigarette butt, still there.

My bookshelves, the music itself, some old commemorative booze bottles, a deer antler, lighters, hats, party souvenirs.

Dust over everything. The dead man's room.

Crazy. I've worked here at this desk in the last year, I don't seem to remember it much, though. Must be too traumatic for me to handle how much I've changed, how much I've left behind.

I don't know how to ask the question any other way, but was I that bad? Look at my stuff, this is the refuse of a partying sedentary guy who likes to listen to music and read books and carry on late into the evening about how wonderful and miraculous it is to have a brain.

That's me, I have the soul of a fat man.

Look at this. Here's my Pat Travers tape. Remember that song "Snortin' Whiskey, Drinkin' Cocaine"? Gets me to rocking out, just thinking about it.

We're snortin' whiskey, and I'm, I'm drinkin' cocaine.
I got this feelin' I'm gonna drive that girl insane.

That's one of the all-time killer-diller heavy metal tunes ever recorded, and just because I can't personally ever again have anything to do with either whiskey or cocaine, that doesn't mean I can't like the *song*.

I can read a murder mystery and not be a murderer, right?

My mind is free to enjoy anything, isn't it?

Imagining a life, though, isn't the same as living one, and perhaps this is what I needed to know about being a writer when I first got into it. If I want to write a novel about down-and-outs and drunks, that doesn't mean I have to be a down-and-out and a drunk. But that's the thing, there's life on the *page*, and there's *life*. I don't want to live the remainder of my time on earth drunk and in a slump. I want to accept my life and embrace my limitations and do the best I can with what time I've got left.

Oh, and here's my videotape of *Barfly* with Mickey Rourke. Betcha I've watched this fifty times. "To all my *friends!*" Remember that? When Mickey Rourke cashes his income-tax refund and goes down to the bar and buys rounds for all his derelict friends, and the hot poetry-review chick is trying to steal him away from Faye Dunaway, and Mickey Rourke's gonna fight Eddie, the bartender, who, Mickey says, "symbolizes everything that disgusts me."

What a flick!

And here's the three books I've published. They're not great books, I guess. They're run-of-the-mill R-rated novels involving alcohol and smoking and other horrible things. When I was writing them, I was most definitely involved in alcohol and smoking and other horrible things, so like, imagine that, life and art were doing the imitation thing. I've never been proud of my books in the I-think-I'm-hot-shit way, but I've always thought it's cool they exist, that I've written them, that a few people have read them. So what am I to say now that I'm no longer that drunken guy who wrote these books? That they're crap?

But I *am* that guy. Hang out with me for a while, listen to me, I talk just like the person talking in those books. My artistic influences and all that good stuff, still the same.

Look at the books on my bookshelf, those I prize, like Prospero once said to Miranda, "above my dukedom."

Kafka, Dostoyevsky, Proust, Beckett, Faulkner, Shake-speare. I like them just as much now as I did before I did my 180-degree turn in life.

Those e.e. cummings poems I used to recite in the bar to impress women— "no one, not even the rain, has such small hands" — or those Shakespeare couplets I used to use— "As the last taste of sweets is sweetest last, / writ in remembrance more than things long past" —the lot of it, I still think it's great.

I've raced a couple of times in Category V, the lowest of the low in terms of bike racing, and I've been thrilled about it, it's been exciting and fun and definitely I posted results worth being proud of—sixth at Hillsboro, ninth at McMinville—but I still have a long way to go if I want to race in Cat IV, which is incredibly fast compared to Cat V. Then if I could post a few good results there, if I could at least hang with the breakaway group in a Cat IV race, and that would be very difficult, I could "cat up" to Cat III, which in bike racing is getting to be a scary level; there are just so many fast people racing Cat III. Cat I and II people, these are the riders who are truly born to the sport—to see them riding, so effortless, so natural in the saddle. The pinnacle is to be a Cat I racer, a true professional bike racer, but then again there are divisions within Cat I, and if, for instance, you're regularly winning professional races in the United States, you might not be worth squat in the European professional bike-racing circuit, you might be dropping back to the team car to fetch water bottles for the real racer, the guy who's ten times better than you.

What I mean is, I used to be a Category I writer, a professional. I obviously haven't done squat in the European pro writer circuit, there's lot of writers who are ten times better than me, and I'm obliged to drop back to the team car of literature and fetch water bottles for the real writers, but, well, darn it, I'm not going to kill myself over it, okay?

See, it's not that *I'm* dead, that my personality has been subsumed into a new reformed and possibly supernatural being, no way, I'm just smaller, I'm just into physical fitness instead of chemical abuse, I'm just older and mellower, I'm a person who has grown tired of being angry and depressed, like everybody else is tired of it, and I've made a series of changes to make myself feel better. And I do feel better. I feel great.

Well, notwithstanding the truck I feel great. I'm trashed physically at this moment, not moving around too well, bending's difficult and walking is and standing up is, but that's *temporary*. Couple-two-three-four weeks, I'll be hammering again. But there's no hurry. I've got time. I can look back over my last year on the bike and finally say what I've been waiting to say to myself the whole time. It's corny, it's cliché, but it's honest: *It's been one hell of a ride, Mike.*

I'm ready to move on with my life now.

Takes me two days because of my slow-motion-injured form of locomotion, but I refile my books and my CDs and cassettes and throw away all the old papers I've got lying around and dust off my desk and my computer and vacuum the ancient ash off the carpet and, like magic, there I am, getting up in the morning, making a pot of coffee, coming here to the computer and using my mind to work again.

I've always wanted to write a crime novel, incidentally, I think since I read *Crime and Punishment,* and I've always wanted to write a novel about a trailer court, and, at least for the last couple of years, I've been wanting to write a novel having to do with cycling. So it starts happening, I'm at my desk every day working on a crime novel set in a trailer court and featuring some folks who ride bicycles— it's totally raunchy R-rated crime comedy or whatever it is, don't matter, though. There are better novelists than me. There are better cyclists than me. There are better professors, fathers, husbands, et cetera. Let them be better.

That's what I've been saying all along. *Accept who you are. Accept that people will be better than you.* This is okay, you don't have to be the best person to be a good person, and all people can reasonably ask of you is that you are a good person.

I gradually get my form back on the bike, too, but we're talking *very* gradually. I'm riding the Litespeed, a titanium bike, extremely sensitive and responsive. The bike feels rickety to me the first few weeks, and I don't care to go fast down a hill or swoop into a corner. But I keep at it, I'm on the road every afternoon again, spinning, working on pedaling in perfect circles, surging, getting out of the saddle, sprinting. Gets so, near the end of July, I've got my strength back, and I've got a new bike, too, a new Trek, a 5500, bought it with the insurance money from the accident.

I guess I'm maybe not as fast as I used to be, not as light, either. A month after the truck hits me, I get on the scale, and I'm weighing 185 pounds.

Get hit by a truck, and gain ten pounds recuperating. Get a load of the irony in *that*.

Of course this additional weight hurts my performance on the road, I can't climb the way I could only five or six weeks ago, I'm lugging an extra full sack of potatoes with me everywhere I ride, but I'm okay with that, I guess. I'm not panicking. I keep riding, keep building up the distance. A person torn down like I've been, that's a person who needs rebuilding, so I'm working on my base mileage, doing sixty and seventy and eighty miles on the weekdays and rides up to 120 miles in hundred-degree heat on Sundays, 350-mile weeks, 400-mile weeks. But I'm not starving myself anymore, not even *thinking* about starving myself anymore. I can't put in mileage like that and try to be on a diet; I need to run my body at equal-in, equal-out fueling. That's the way I ride the bike best, that's the way I think best.

I'm rising early again, too, before dawn every day, and I'm writing again. Five or six or seven hours a day, I'm at it.

When the fall term begins, I disregard the scene that accompanies it. I stay away.

I have narrowed down what I want to do in this world, what I feel is real, what I feel I can manage in my do-the-best-I-can way. I'm really a writer, I'm really a cyclist, I'm really a professor, I'm really a family man, and in order to be even half-assed at these things, well, I'm too busy to hang out at the fall socials and meet people and watch them get drunk and stumble around and argue with each other. I am not doing anybody any good by standing around and talking.

When I worked in the factory years ago, this line was a classic: "Let's have a little less talk and a little more work, people."

I've got to lay that one on my students, see what they think.

I get out on group ride, and start getting dropped again. Not badly dropped. Somebody might break on me up a climb, and I'll start charging to close the gap, and when it seems like catching that wheel is going to break me, I allow the effort to break me, and I sit up and call off hostilities. I'm riding because I like to ride, not because I want my eyeballs to explode in the process of chasing down one of my *friends* and proving what to them? That I can climb better over a two-hundred-foot stretch of road than them? And do this one time out of *two*?

Truth be told, I feel more sluggish, thicker, less nimble, and I worry maybe I'm like the cycling version of the guy in *Flowers for Algernon*. Remember that guy? Took that drug and got really, really genius-level smart, only to have the drug wear off and end up not too bright again. It could be me who lost a ton of weight and climbed like an angel on the bike for a couple of months there, only to collide with a truck and have the weight gradually spread back on and end up being that big guy getting spit off the back of group ride on a rainy night.

On the other hand, I'm still riding three hundred miles a week. If I'm a few pounds heavier than I was in the spring, so what? It's not like I'm fat and out of shape, because a fat and out-of-shape person can't ride three hundred miles a week.

Cycling is my form of recreation. I am re-creating myself, making myself new. A few pounds either way, it's not worth losing sleep over.

*Keep at it*, I tell my students. *You will never make it*, I say, *if you quit trying*. I say, *You must accept who you are, that there is no best person, only people who are doing the best they can.*

So many rules, so many ways of expressing the same thing, which is this: Having a good life is like learning to ride a bicycle. Once you learn how to stay upright and pedal, you will never forget how. What's important is that if you stray away from the bike of your life, if you are injured or drunk or sick or otherwise preoccupied, you will always know that you can get back on your bike again and ride.

*Find joy in this,* I tell my students, *and never give up hope.*

# 19

$Y$ep. They say if you met yourself on the street you wouldn't know yourself. If I looked around and saw *my*self, a year ago, when I was thirty-nine, two hundred pounds and rolling around the parking lot of the Lenoir Mall in the rain, a half an hour before the start of the Bridge to Bridge Incredible Cycling Challenge, I wouldn't know myself. Not at all. I didn't know myself *then*, for then, I was looking back at myself at thirty-*eight* years old, two hundred *fifty-five* pounds and a heavy smoker and a heavy drinker and, despite this, rolling around the roads south of Carbondale, trying to stay within sight of Saki on group ride, _____

when we were hammering on a route known as Rocky Comfort or when we were climbing the Smiley Face hill out of Makanda to U.S. Highway 51.

If I had heard, at thirty-eight, at 255 pounds, that in one year I would be weighing only two hundred pounds and participating in the Bridge to Bridge, I never would have believed it.

If I had heard, at thirty-nine, at two hundred pounds, that in one year I would be rolling around the Lenoir Mall parking lot, at forty, at 180, and feeling way too heavy for this event, I most definitely would have gotten angry.

I was so proud, at thirty-nine, at two hundred pounds, of having lost fifty-five pounds and having improved so much on the bike and done so much to rectify the embarrassment I felt when I appeared butt-naked and riding in the rain in *Gentleman's Quarterly*, which is the exact same embarrassment I've felt about my weight my whole life. *Mike*, the thirty-nine-year-old me would have said looking at the forty-year-old me, *you weigh 180 pounds, you've done a complete 180-degree turn in your life, and you've made it, dude, what on earth have you got to complain about?*

Only this. No one in recovery ever recovers. That's why they call it *in recovery*, meaning it's ongoing, it's not over yet, there is no endgame to recovery.

I can tell you today, at forty years old, rolling around the Lenoir Mall parking lot a half an hour before the start of the Bridge to Bridge, my second year here at the event, that my quality of life is the best it's ever been.

# HEFT ON WHEELS

I've made some incredible major positive strides forward, but I'm not going to tell you everything's perfect. There's much, much work yet to do—on the bike, with my career, with my family, my personal relationships—and in order to do work of any sort, with any degree of competence, a person needs to be self-critical, not in a destructive way but in a way that generates the motivation to continue improving.

It's not winning that matters, it's the motivation to continue improving.

This year's version of the Bridge to Bridge will be a lot more pleasant than last year's, I can tell you that. The weather's magnificent, skies clear, temps nice, wind non-threatening. A few minutes now till the start, and we're lining up, 750 of us, behind a squad car that will lead us out of the parking lot and onto the road to our destinies. When the squad car turns on its cherries and gives one blast of the siren, that's when we'll clip into our pedals and in a great wash of gears and wheels we'll begin rolling together toward the mountains. All that climbing and hurt ahead of us. All that training we've brought here to take along with us. All that history we have with bikes, with people, with our hearts.

Every cyclist accepts the responsibility to pedal a great weight uphill. A very small cyclist, like Saki was or like my friend Don the psychologist is, you may think of this person's 135 pounds as no great weight, but to the

135-pound cyclist climbing a mountain, 135 pounds is a great weight indeed. Likewise, 180 pounds, compared to 255 pounds, may seem like an extremely slight weight.

See what I'm saying? A human being on a bicycle is by definition, by laws of physics, a heft on wheels. Could be me, could be you, could be any weight we carry, we're all rolling in the same direction.

The squad car's cherries come on, the siren blasts one time, and the squad starts moving. A great wash of noise follows, a rush of cyclists clipping in and gearing up and straining toward the future, and we're all together in this, it's time to go, go, go.

*Allez, allez, allez.*

*Vite, vite.*

*Allons-y.*

# ABOUT THE AUTHOR

Mike Magnuson teaches creative writing at Southern Illinois University and has written for *Esquire*, *GQ*, and *Bicycling*. He is the author of two novels, *The Right Man for the Job* and *The Fire Gospels*, as well as the memoir, *Lummox*.